PRAISE FOR
A JOURNEY OF SEA AND STONE

"Which books keep you sane when the world locks you down? For me it's those with marrow-deep ties to the geography they describe—Wendell Berry's Port William stories, Timothy Egan's pilgrimage to Rome, Henry Beston's year on the beach at Cape Cod. New to this heartening shelf is Tracy Balzer's *A Journey of Sea and Stone*, the tale of her longstanding love for the cloistered island of Iona, off the Scottish coast. We all have places we seem to have known forever. In lucid, rhythmic prose, Balzer develops a spiritual travelogue of solace and gratitude, of openness to wonder and reason, and of a longing for what Beston called 'the dear earth itself underfoot.' This is a welcome book."

—Leif Enger, author of *Peace Like a River*

"A visionary, Tracy Balzer draws us in to a vivid sense of what holiness looks like, feels like. She demonstrates how anyone who experiences this transformative power can never again be the same—it is that radical."

—Luci Shaw, Writer in Residence, Regent College, and author of *The Generosity* and *Eye of the Beholder*

"This book is about listening and looking and learning; it is about being deeply there to hear the heartbeat of a place, and the teaching that comes from all these things is gracious and generous. This work is like a polished serpentine stone from St. Columba's Bay on Iona: hold it to the light and you find more every time you look."

—Kenneth Steven, author and poet

"The ancient tradition of spiritual pilgrimage reminds us that ordinary places can be holy places. Tracy Balzer takes us to the holy Isle of Iona to find fresh inspiration and meaning in our daily lives. If you want a spiritual pilgrimage that will renew your faith, you don't have to travel far. All you have to do is read this book!"

—Dr. Winfield Bevins, director of church planting at Asbury Seminary and author of *Ever Ancient, Ever New*

"Tracy Balzer has given us all a wonderful gift. She invites us into sacred spaces and reminds us that we, on our own soulful journeys, are on holy ground."

—Brent Bill, author of *Holy Silence: The Gift of Quaker Spirituality*

"The real gift of Balzer's book is learning that our ordinary lives and receptive hearts can become sacred 'islands' in their own right as we create sanctuaries for ourselves and one another."

—Lisa Deam, author of *3000 Miles to Jesus: Pilgrimage as a Way of Life for Spiritual Seekers*

A JOURNEY

of SEA

AND STONE

A JOURNEY

of SEA

AND STONE

HOW HOLY PLACES GUIDE
and RENEW US

TRACY
BALZER

BROADLEAF BOOKS
MINNEAPOLIS

Cover image: Shutterstock
Cover design: Gearbox
Interior artwork: Paul Soupiset | Soupiset Design

Print ISBN: 978-1-5064-6459-6
eBook ISBN: 978-1-5064-6460-2

For my granddaughter,
Lizzy Iona

CONTENTS

CONTENTS

FOREWORD

The last time I moved across the country I had to start building a relationship with the trees.

I grew up in a little town called Mukilteo, about thirty miles north of Seattle in the Pacific Northwest of the United States, which means I grew up with large trees. Sure, pine and fir trees were around, but what is embedded in my very being are the cedar trees. Tall and looming, reaching up to the heavens, the Empire State Buildings of the forest foliage. They have a distinct reddish interior underneath their flaky bark, which juxtaposes pleasingly against the forever green landscape.

Cedar trees aren't great climbing trees. Their limbs begin too high off the ground. But that doesn't mean they remain strangers to the local inhabitants. They provide shelter from the never-ending rain. They provide a buffer from the battering wind storms that rip through the neighborhoods every now and then. Although some, if it's their time, fall to the earth from which they grew, and we all pray that their descent isn't stopped prematurely by a parked car or a family house.

To live in the Pacific Northwest is to dwell with the trees. We've built society around them. We've built society from them. They are the source material in which we build our homes. We sleep in the trees just like the squirrels and ravens do. They are the source material for our furniture. They hold us just like the slugs and the mountain lion. They give us warmth in our hearth. They provide a way to tell our story, best exampled by the indigenous communities who erected totem poles throughout the area, carved from the bodies of red cedars. They, in a way, remind you of who you are.

I've lived most of my life in the Northwest, but just recently my family moved to Austin, Texas. We moved right at the beginning of the coronavirus pandemic, meaning we moved to a new community when that community had become unavailable. Distanced. Sheltered in place. Closed and unavailable. It's weird to move to a bustling city where the bustle has been put on hold for the foreseeable future. All of our normal ways of connection had gone away. Restaurants, parks, churches, schools, festivals . . .

all on hold for the good of all. Even our friends here had some complications, so our first month was just us holed up in a rental house with not much to do except to go on neighborhood walks.

It was on these walks that I began my relationship with the central Texas oak tree.

If a cedar's ambition is to reach the heavens, the oak tree's ambition is to open its arms as wide as possible. It's a loving gesture, actually, because to survive a central Texas summer is to find where the shade is. Oak trees are masters of shade. Their limbs grow unbelievably long. They splinter out like the spiderweb crack in your windshield, sometimes even touching the ground and raising up again for another go at winning the long-distance medal. They are amazing climbing trees, as my kids have discovered. They are also an amazing place to talk with a friend, or have a meal, or take a much-needed nap.

I didn't know this at first. The oak tree was a stranger to me, and I to it. To begin a homestead in a new place is to start a conversation with the landscape. I felt like a stranger for a long time because I didn't know what the oak trees had to say about me. Who I was and where I was connected to the universe. And frankly, I didn't know what I could share about them. We had only had quick pleasantries in times past when I had visited Austin as a tourist. Now we were neighbors. And we've had so much to talk about since I moved into the neighborhood.

This book before you is about a deep and long conversation that has happened between humans throughout time and a little island off the coast of what we now call Scotland. The Iona landscape has the ingredients that all landscapes possess—its own unique characteristics that imbue individuality "in the family of things," as Mary Oliver puts it. Every place has its wonders and glories. This isn't an argument for which place is better.

This is a witness about the particular conversation that this landscape has excavated out of human lives for centuries. What makes Iona sacred is not necessarily the ecosystem that has evolved on this isolated island, but the way in which this ecosystem has hosted soul care in the lives of all who show up on her shores. Tracy Balzer is our insightful guide, bearing witness to this particular transformation, yes, but then also pointing us to the rhythms and practices that we can implement in any landscape we find ourselves in. What makes this book so powerful is her continued participation in landscape transformation. This is the holy transformation she is inviting us into in the pages of this book.

Good journey to you.

Scott Erickson
scottericksonart.com
@scottthepainter

INTRODUCTION

Why Iona?

> When in some future time I shall sit in a madly
> crowded assembly with music and dancing round
> me, and the wish arises to retire in to the loneli-
> est loneliness, I shall think of Iona.
>
> —Felix Mendelssohn, 1829

In 1997, two of my favorite authors, Luci Shaw and
Madeleine L'Engle, collaborated on a book called
Friends for the Journey. In it they each reflected on
their long-term friendship and how they encouraged each other as writers and women of faith. As
a mother of young children and an aspiring writer
myself, I delighted in being a mouse in their corner,
listening in on their amusing anecdotes and insights
about creativity, spirituality, and friendship. The book
even included recipes they'd shared over the years, as
cooking and eating together were part of the fabric of

their friendship. I tried one of those recipes, which had I dog-eared years ago, just the other night, and the results were delicious.

There are many things in their book I've found to be delicious. (When writing provides food for my soul, I can't help but describe it as *delicious*.) One such delicacy is a poem written by Shaw that changed the course of my spiritual life and brought me to a new sense of the significance of sacred places. For some reason beyond Shaw's skill as a poet, this poem palpably carved itself into my subconscious, where its imagery and vision sat dormant for years.

The poem is called "The Holiness of Iona." When I read it for the first time, I was in my midthirties, with no clue what or where Iona was. But I knew I had to find out:

> How our Celtic blood stirred as we
> navigated along the single car track
> across Mull, westward between the purplish hills,
> under the torn cloth of clouds and then
> over the final channel, its green-gray waves
> chipping away at the hull of the ferry.
> The buffet of sea-wind felt rough
> as the breath of God. We could hardly wait

to settle in, to inhale
the holy island's scent of sanctity.

The first stanza of the poem cast the vision of a holy journey, traveling far over an unfamiliar landscape and across the sea . . . to an island. It captured me. Growing up landlocked in Colorado, it wasn't until my college years in Seattle that I had the chance to meet the ocean personally. When I did, I was smitten; the two of us bonded immediately. The imagery in this poem—the movement of waves and wind—was instantly appealing, inviting me to virtually join Shaw and her friends as they sailed across the Sound of Iona, the "final channel," to a holy island, sustained by the breath of God.

More than fifteen hundred years ago, an Irish monk named Columba (also known as Columcille) left Ireland for an unknown destination. Columba was born and raised as the Celtic expression of Christianity was thriving in Ireland, and it nurtured in him the deep conviction that was characteristic of the Christian Celts in the centuries immediately following the days of St. Patrick. A man of great passion and vision, Columba responded to what he believed to be God's calling by leaving all he'd ever known—his beloved home, his lively ministry, and his identity as a son of nobility. He chose twelve friends to join him, and together they set out from what is now Northern Ireland, intent on finding a new land where they might begin a Christian community.

Their primitive boat carried them to the north and east—less than two hundred miles as the crow flies—and they landed on the tiny island of Iona, one of the dozens of small islands known today as the Inner Hebrides of Scotland. Somehow, they managed to eke out a life, knit together by their faith and commitment to each other as they faced potentially formidable foes, whether in the forces of nature or in the power of marauding invaders. In spite of it all, Columba's monastery thrived and became the area's primary center for Christian learning and mission, sending community members from their small island out into mainland Scotland to spread the light of the gospel.

According to one of his biographers, Columba and his fellow monks "had a deep understanding of the human predicament of alienation, self-doubt and separation from God and from other people. They responded with a programme of healing which tackled the whole person, body, mind and soul, and which

4

was predicated on the need for repeated forgiveness and assurance of acceptance by God." Columba's insight and leadership as a saint and a scholar put Iona on the map as a holy place, a sacred space.

And while the world has changed dramatically over the more than fifteen hundred years since Columba lived on Iona, this vision for humanity remains. Visitors who make the long trek there inevitably come away with a new sense of the holy. This is the "scent of sanctity" that can appeal to our wounded world and to my own wounded soul:

And it was all so lovely—the sea
between the rocks a clear bottle green over
white sand. Vivid cottage gardens
cloistered beyond the jetty,
bordered with delphiniums, rank with
nasturtiums. Scores of eager day-trippers
with their back-packs and bikes crowded
the block-topped path of the Abbey;
tourists laced the air with
syllables we struggled to recognize.
The craft shops, with their local pottery
and Celtic jewelry. The gift shops, even in
the Abbey—bookmarks, scarves
like butterflies, key rings, postcards.

With appealing imagery, the poem invites me: sea, rocks, bottle green, white sand, cottage gardens, cloistered, delphiniums, nasturtiums—each of them a compelling invitation tapping into our innate desire for the original garden, the glories of Creation pronounced "good" by their Creator. That desire is real. Creation feels many times like it is broken: raging wild fires, violent hurricanes, systemic racism, and a global pandemic all threaten our sense of security or stability.

But in the midst of this brokenness, there is substantial beauty, reminding me of God's creative and redemptive work. This is work that has been done in the past and will continue if humanity chooses to collaborate. To read the work of a poet like Luci Shaw or Mary Oliver, or my friend Kenneth Steven, is to be challenged to engage in that good work again. The artwork of Makoto Fujimura or Georgia O'Keefe restores my hope in the role that humanity can play in the restoration of the world. The musical mastery of Edward Elgar or Aretha Franklin reconnects me with the numinous, the transcendent.

To lean into beauty is to submit to transformation, fueled by the power of a creative God. And our transformation can in turn transform a broken Creation:

We'd expected to find Columcille,
and Patrick—the ancient saints
blessing us with a benediction
of solitude, with a peace that drops
like fading light behind the rocks.
All we sensed was . . . an absence. We all
missed something. We all said that we missed it—
like the wild gold of the iris blooms
whose dark summer leaves hugged
the creases of the island, their spring boldness
faded to a single wilted rag here, there.

Here the poet grounds us in truth To desire a meaningful encounter with God in a place like Iona is good; the problem comes when we expect it to come about in a *particular way*. Great saints have indeed walked Iona's paths, prayed there, performed miracles there, even given their lives there. Iona is known as a sacred place for a reason.

But we don't get to determine how God will speak. Instead, we are invited to engage in the active spiritual practice of paying attention, of taking notice of what God has to say *in God's way*. This posture of humility makes us more open to the transforming presence of God, wherever we might find ourselves. It is wisdom to stand, watch, wait, and listen:

Later, a walk together across the
Close-cropped velvet and up
Over the backbone of rock to a bay pebbly
As Galilee, a meal of fish
And soda-bread. An evening prayer
In the guest room, small as a cell,
Showed us where to look, how to see: Our
High anticipation had detoured us
Away from holiness, and when we least
Expected it, there it was, God's felt presence
In our human trinity of longing.

I can certainly identify with that cogent phrase "detoured . . . away from holiness." To be detoured is rarely perceived as a positive thing. We all know the sinking feeling that comes when our navigation app announces, "Recalculating." We have taken a wrong turn.

Yet this is par for our spiritual course. We are regularly derailed, sometimes due to circumstances beyond our control but perhaps most often due to our own inability to know "where to look, how to see." The gift of a place like Iona—and of sacred spaces the world over—is that it helps us pay closer attention to what God is doing and how the Spirit may be calling us. This means learning *where to look and how to see.* It means taking time apart from all that is demanding in my life so I can grow in attention to holiness, to beauty, to relationships. It's telling that at the end of the Iona poem, for Luci Shaw and her friends, the deepest holiness was perceived in friendship, their "trinity of longing." The presence of God is perhaps seen most keenly in human relationships.

Shaw's beautiful description of her experience on Iona planted a seed of curiosity that grew silently in me for years. Then, in the spring of 2000, the university I work at asked me and my husband, Cary, to lead a summer study program in Ireland. The "Iona file" I'd been keeping in my brain was immediately opened. I promptly found an available weekend in our Ireland itinerary and made a plan to sail over to Scotland. Iona was calling, and I had to go.

Now, twenty years later, I am preparing for my group of twenty souls to travel together on a pilgrimage next July. I have guided a whole slew of Christian pilgrims to this sacred island over the years, eager to share its holiness, beauty, and call to attentiveness with others. This happens every summer, so perhaps you'll feel the nudge to come along. But even if you never make it to Iona, it's possible to learn from it, to virtually allow its essence to seep into your soul and change your perspective.

As you read this book, I hope you'll see how this island has become a spiritual director to me, and that you'll consider the sacred spaces that have served in such a way for you. Perhaps it will leave you with the realization that you also need such a place of deep connection with God, perhaps more local to you.

I have been fortunate to have wise spiritual friends and directors in my life. Some I've met with personally and regularly, some I've learned from less frequently and at a distance, and some I've only known through their writing. If you have ever met with a spiritual director, you know that it's not their job to give you a checklist of spiritual tasks to accomplish or a surefire method of growing closer to God. Rather, they seek to awaken in you the sense of your own uniqueness as a beloved child of God and then gently help you discern where God may be at work in your life. This is a ministry intended to protect you from the dangers of a spiritual echo chamber, where you hear only your own voice . . . a fearsome prospect.

If you are seeking a deeper spiritual life, it's wise to turn to others for guidance. A good spiritual director provides this kind of guidance by asking you thoughtful, reflective questions, the kind that encourage contemplation about how God may be at work. I've structured this book around three of those important questions, which Iona has helped me articulate:

Where is God? Spiritual directors help you sort out all the sounds, all the voices in your life in order to hear the truest Voice. They ask about the meaningful ways you connect with God and about the ways you might feel far from God or near to God.

Who am I? They will ask you questions about where you find your identity, whether you feel you are moving away from God or closer to him, how God is shaping and challenging you, and what your deepest fears are and how you can confront them.

What can I offer the world? Spiritual direction can help you see how God is nudging you into your true vocation by helping you see the ways you are uniquely gifted, how you can stretch and grow into deeper meaning and purpose, and what you have to give to the world.

It is a recurring prayer in my life that God would provide such directors for me. How astonishing and strange it is that God has answered that prayer through an island. Throughout this book, I'll reveal how Iona has helped me and others respond to these three questions of spiritual direction and how those insights help me live more faithfully in the world even when I'm far away from the spiritual beauty of the place.

You will likely notice some curious nomenclature in some of the chapter titles, thanks to the colorful Scots language that has woven its way into my Iona experience. Stick with it—I think you'll find those Scots words a delightful addition to your vocabulary, as I have.

At the end of each chapter, you'll also find a few questions for spiritual direction. I hope they will lead you into deeper reflection on your own faith. The aim of this book is to use the beauty and historical significance of holy places to nurture a curious, growing hunger for more authenticity in our spiritual lives.

We recognize that need, deep in our souls, because we have felt the unseen wind, that mysterious hint that God is near and up to something . . . something God wants us to be a part of. This gradual attuning of our ear is ongoing, a lifetime project as the Holy Spirit quickens our spirit to notice God.

I
WHERE IS GOD?

1

A SACRED ISLAND

My soul thirsts for God, for the living God.
When can I go and meet with God?

—Psalm 42:2

One of the clearest memories I have of visiting Iona for the first time is leaving it.

At the end of my three-day introduction to the sacred isle, I reluctantly walked up the ferry ramp and handed my ticket to a gentleman wearing a neon-yellow vest. The Caledonian MacBrayne ferry is the only option for taking nonlocal folks back and forth between Iona and the whimsically named village of Fionnphort on the Isle of Mull.

I wanted to get one last look at the island as we pulled away, so I purposefully made my way to the ferry's upper deck, only to find that someone had beaten me to the best spot. An old man stood there, wearing a full-length black habit and a boxy black hat, his chin sporting a grizzled gray beard. I surmised he was a member of the Orthodox clergy—Russian or Greek, I had no way to know. I settled into the second-best viewing spot right behind him.

As our small ferry pulled away from the jetty, all aboard fixed our attention on Iona's shoreline: the village with its line of charming cottages, the historic Argyll Hotel where I had stayed, and the gray, stately Iona Abbey, staring back solemnly as if to say, "Do not forget what you have heard."

Indeed, I had heard some important, life-shaping things on my first visit to Iona. One was that I was more capable than I thought myself to be. It is not easy to get to Iona, and in the year 2000, I did not have a smartphone to help redirect me should I get on the wrong train, ferry, or bus. It was a two-day journey on at least six different vehicles, but I miraculously checked into the Argyll Hotel on Iona precisely on time. I felt quite proud of myself.

More importantly, I learned how greatly my soul needed silence and solitude. For three carefree days, I had space to breathe, to walk, to pray, and to sit and gaze at the beauty I found at every turn. As a full-time campus minister and mother of two young children, it had been many years since I'd had three *hours* of such contemplation, much less three days.

From the top deck of the ferry, I watched curiously as the old man, a holy man, raised his hand deliberately and made the sign of the cross over Iona. His motion served as a full stop, a period at the end of a declarative sentence: *Iona is a sacred place.*

No, I would not forget.

Within each of us is a longing for the sacred. Blaise Pascal famously claimed that humans possess an "infinite abyss" that "can be filled only with an infinite and immutable object; in other words by God himself." The wise writer who penned the biblical book of Ecclesiastes claimed that God has "set eternity in the human heart; yet no one can fathom what God has done from beginning to end" (Ecclesiastes 3:11). Humans are created with the knowledge of the sacred, even if it is an incomplete understanding.

All great art, the truly imaginative work of humans, challenges us to see beyond what is right in front of us. It's why a symphonic suite like Holst's *The Planets* is often described as transcendent. Or why viewers stand transfixed before the works of

Van Gogh or Rembrandt, looking "through" the painting rather than merely "at" it. Or how a virtual visit to Middle Earth via book or film calls us higher up and deeper into a place that is "beyond."

We all yearn for that place beyond. Ross Wilson is an internationally known sculptor and artist from Belfast, Northern Ireland. One of his best-loved creations is a sculpture of a smartly dressed man reaching to open the door of the wardrobe that stands before him. Wilson was commissioned to create it in honor of the hundredth anniversary of the birth of C. S. Lewis, who was born and grew up in East Belfast, not far from where the statue now stands.

As I contemplate our desire for the sacred, Wilson's sculpture provides a hint. Anyone who has been transported into the world of Narnia via Lewis's classic books knows that it is the wardrobe that makes that journey possible, serving as a portal, a doorway from the ordinary world into a magical one. Last semester, the campus where I work as a minister hosted Wilson as a visiting speaker, and his works were displayed in the university gallery. Over coffee one morning, he related that, with very few exceptions, children will walk up to his sculpture and try to open the wardrobe door; *they want to go inside.* This is not a surprise to me; we all want to go inside! Any lover of the Chronicles of Narnia, regardless of age, wants to believe that what Lewis called "the deeper magic" might exist after all.

Imaginative art connects us to that which is transcendent, to the Creator of all that is good and beautiful. It's one of many ways the desire for sacred places is nurtured in us. And Iona is one of those sacred places, one that speaks to our longing for what is beyond.

Iona is known as a "thin place," where the dividing line between heaven and earth can seem as thin as tissue paper. Its deep-rootedness in the Celtic Christian story and its exquisite natural setting give me space to listen to the voice of God and to my own soul; it draws me into a way of longing for God. Prior to that first visit to Iona, I would have said that for the greater part of my forty years on earth, I had truly loved Jesus and desired to *follow* him. Now, after many visits, Iona, in its mysterious way, has made me *desire* him. It was and continues to be a palpable sensation, a holy longing for God.

Lewis famously talked about this predicament as homesickness for a land we've never seen and yet instinctively know is where we belong, the only place that can be the source of true joy. In his novel *Till We Have Faces*, Lewis uses the character of Psyche to describe this universal longing by way of analogy: "It almost hurt me . . . like a bird in a cage when the other birds of its kind are flying home . . . to find the place where all the beauty came from—my country, the place where I ought to have been born. The longing for *home*."

This longing lies within each of us; we are created with it. It may lie dormant for many years, decades even, until something or someone wakes us up: Scripture, Creation, a friend, a good book, maybe even an island. Sacred places like Iona give us a hint of our true home through the stories they tell. The history of a place, the significant events that took place there, contribute to a sense of sanctity. Equally important are the holy people who lived in such places—apostles, saints, priests, missionaries—who lived and walked and even did miraculous things.

The tiny island of Iona in the Inner Hebrides of Scotland has a history so momentous in the Christian story that we risk hyperbole when we recount it. *How the Irish Saved Civilization* is not only the title of Thomas Cahill's best-selling book; it could easily serve as a definitive statement about the role that

Iona played in history, grandiose as it may sound. The "Irish" Cahill refers to includes Columba and his band of monks, who apparently possessed this desire for the sacred in addition to a healthy dose of wanderlust. They had read of the ascetic life of the Desert Fathers in Egypt, and this inspired many of them to seek out a "desert" of their own—a remote and lonely place where their service to God would be undeterred. The wild and windswept isle of Iona, just three miles long and one mile wide, would become their "desert." For the better part of the next six centuries, a monastic community would be present on Iona.

An oft-cited prophecy attributed to Columba (though its true author is unknown) makes a claim worth pondering:

Iona of my heart, Iona of my love,
Instead of monks' voices shall be
the lowing of cattle;
But ere the world shall come
to an end,
Iona shall be as it was.

This prediction—that the audible voices of monks would not always be heard on Iona—proved to be true. In the centuries following Columba's death in 597, his monastery was repeatedly attacked by Viking marauders who plundered its treasures and eventually destroyed the place altogether. Even so, their words echo throughout history, speaking through the glorious illuminated manuscripts they left behind, the most famous of which is the Book of Kells. Later, Benedictine monks occupied the space where Columba's monastery stood and speak today through the ruins of the now restored abbey. Its ancient walls reverberate with the prayers of those who have gone before, expressed in stained glass images of Celtic saints like Columba, Patrick, and Brigid. Their bold proclamation of truth remains in the intricately carved high crosses that stand in front of the abbey, a visual narrative of biblical history. To be on Iona is to experience a deep silence, simultaneously mingled with the voices of the saints of the past.

> Sacred places, wherever they might be, are made sacred by sacrificial living and dying, especially when both are an expression of a deeply held faith. Such places ask us to stop and listen and patiently wait for those ancient lives to speak.

Sacred places, wherever they might be, share this distinction. They are made sacred by sacrificial living and dying, especially when both are expressions of a deeply held faith. Such places ask us to stop and listen, focus our eyes intently, and patiently wait for those ancient lives to speak. We are invited to learn and receive by purposefully reading, investigating, and pondering the ancient texts, particularly those from the Bible. By examining the lives of the great saints of old, we may be surprised to find the courage and conviction in their lives spilling over into our own.

There is also something about encountering these "voices" that resonates with us internally. Many of us recognize a natural inclination within ourselves to walk in the footsteps of the great saints and influencers of history. Like the late congressman John Lewis and others, do you find the idea of crossing the Edmund Pettus Bridge in Selma, Alabama, ennobling? Or do you imagine running your finger along the carved names of soldiers on the Vietnam Memorial in Washington, DC? Do you desire to visit the Holy Land and walk in the footsteps of Jesus?

The world turns and changes. The audible voices of monks, saints, and the great bridge crossers evaporate, but they leave behind treasures for us to discover, spiritual nourishment for our souls so that we might continue on the good path. Their voices linger in these sacred places, inviting us farther up and deeper in.

In the frantic pace of our daily lives, we often fret about not having enough time . . . and then we whine about being bored when it feels we have too much of it. No matter how many planners or apps we employ to get a handle on it, we can't seem to feel anything but behind. Time can feel like an enemy, especially if we crave deep, spiritual reflection on what is most important. The crowded, noisy spaces most of us inhabit are not conducive to that reflection or to prayer.

On Iona, there are no movie theaters or fast-food restaurants, no stoplights. Even the internet is not reliable. Whenever I offer this description of Iona, the response is almost always an amusing one: *Why would anyone want to spend their vacation time going somewhere that has . . . nothing?* It is true that on Iona there is less of everything, which means there is more space for what we truly need if we hope to attend to our sense of "home," our deep longing for the things of God.

Sacred places like Iona offer the one thing we cannot seem to grasp in our hyperproductive culture: unstructured time. And that is a true gift for the weary soul. The New Testament cites two Greek terms for time: *chronos* and *kairos*. *Chronos*—as the word implies—is linear, with a beginning and an end, measurable in minutes and hours, weeks and months, centuries and epochs. We can't read a book without thinking chrono-logically. This is how we grasp the passing of our earthly days as well: we had a beginning, the day of our birth, and one day we will experience the end, the last day of the *chronos* of a life.

Kairos, however, cannot be contained by a one-dimensional calendar or clock. It doesn't have a straightforward "before" and "after" or "beginning" and "end." *Kairos* is God's time. It is the time and way in which God fulfills his purpose. In the Gospels, when John the Baptist tells his followers that "the kingdom of heaven has come near" (Matthew 3:2), he is talking about *kairos*, when what God wants done is done. *Kairos* reveals that through Christ, a whole new way of understanding time has entered the world: it is time that is characterized not by dates and calendars but by the will of a God who is working to make all things new.

Because arriving on Iona is such a visceral experience, this particular sense of time is one of the first things I notice. I feel the pressure of *chronos* slide off of me like old skin that needs to be shed. On Iona I experience time in a dramatically different way than I do in my everyday life; time there seems multidimensional. The simple fact of being rid of the pressures of being constantly connected and accessible adds a dimension of true freedom to life. Rarely have I witnessed anyone in a hurry on Iona, and rarely have I been in a hurry when I am there. The pace at which we live our lives is an indicator of the inner condition of our souls, and Iona insistently points this out to me.

Along with the awareness that time moves differently on Iona comes a deep quietude that is freely available on the island. Even in the height of summer, when scores of tourists come for the day, I still manage to find my own private space on the beach. (Correction: I often have the beach entirely to myself.) The only sounds I hear are seabirds and wild geese flying overhead and the calming rhythm of waves and wind. Ewes are bleating in the distance, calling for their lambs. These natural sounds melt into the kind of silence that seems elusive in my daily life. There is the mechanical hum of the dishwasher or clothes dryer, or the *clang-clang* of farm vehicles bouncing along our rutted street, or the insistent buzzing of my phone, or the whining of my dog, who is adorable but insists that I be the recipient of her requests.

I can't complain. I live in a semirural area where deer greet us regularly and a herd of cows munches contentedly in the field behind our house. It's nothing like the high-energy sounds of an urban setting. But where silence is concerned, everything is relative. It's not only the external volume that can overwhelm but our own internal noise. The stressful thoughts and fearful imaginings that populate my internal landscape are so loud at times that I might just as well be in Times Square on New Year's Eve. Sometimes I long to escape to Iona just to stifle the abundant noise that fills my inner and outer worlds.

The peace I experience on the island comes not from the absence of conflict but from a shalom of true inner and outer flourishing. The peace that we obtain in sacred places is something we can take back with us into the world and set loose like a thousand colorful balloons into an empty sky.

I experience this kind of shalom most profoundly as I interact with other people on Iona, most of whom I do not know and likely will not ever see again. We greet each other with a smile on the walking path. We worship together in the abbey every evening. There exists an unspoken agreement that while we are all here together on this fleck of green land floating in the Atlantic, we are not about to let ideologies or theological differences harm the shalom of a holy moment.

Sacred places like Iona often have a way of recalibrating our lives—the pace at which we move, the ways we choose to spend our time and money, and the ideas that call for our attention. This is especially noted where monastic life has been or is being lived out. While the historic Columban and Benedictine monasteries on Iona ceased existing many centuries ago, the rhythm of daily prayer and worship remains, led each morning and evening in the abbey by the members of the Iona Community. Each day the bells of the abbey ring, morning and night, prodding me to stop what I'm doing and be present to the God who is very near. The rhythm of entering the abbey sanctuary each day for prayer anchors me in a most life-giving way.

Of all the charming souvenirs that routinely tempt me in the Scottish isles, it is this sacred rhythm that is my most valuable keepsake. Iona has taught me that the regular spiritual practice of stillness before God is what gives me life. It is what takes me from chaos to *kairos*. But eventually, I have to leave Iona and come home.

This essential rhythm comes under forceful attack the moment I set foot on US soil. The transition from the peace of Iona to the frantic pace of modern living is jarring: long lines of impatient travelers at the airport, the stress of the customs process, the dramatic reacquaintance with the speed of cars on the freeway. I may have only been gone for two weeks, but I feel I've entered a foreign country rather than the one of my birth. The external demands of modern culture don't have much patience for the internal rhythms that have been cultivated on a remote island.

I am well aware that merging these two realities will be a battle, yet too often the forces of busyness and productivity overcome my desire for a healthier rhythm that is supported by regular engagement with God in the same silence and solitude I find on Iona. Even though I know good and well that a rhythm of silence, in my own sacred space, is what my soul most needs, it is the very thing I most easily sacrifice. The result is a disordered pattern of higher levels of anxiety and stress. And that is not the way I want to live.

It took going to Iona, to a sacred place, to show me the importance of rhythm for my soul. So when I am home, I know that my best days are also rooted in that rhythm, and that begins with finding a sacred place of my own right where I am. In the spring and summer, that is likely to be my front porch.

Our porch faces due east, just like the Argyll Hotel on Iona. Instead of gazing out on the Sound of Iona and its calming waters, I sit on my porch in Arkansas and watch the myriad of colorful birds that visit our trees and feeders: red-bellied woodpeckers, goldfinches, cardinals, indigo buntings, and hummingbirds en masse. On other days, I opt for the tartan-upholstered chair in my home office, a space I've intentionally made as unoffice-like as possible by adorning it with the images and colors of Iona.

I claim my own sacred space. For twenty or thirty minutes, whether surrounded by birdsong or the quiet of my home office, I still my heart and mind and listen for the voice of God. I tend to draw upon the Psalms for wisdom, as that ancient prayer book is so instructive when it comes to conversing with God. And always there are the essential elements of stillness and silence.

The rhythm that sacred places offer us, whether on a remote island or our front porch, can serve us well as we seek a healthier order to our lives. Taking regular time, daily, for quiet meditation is one of the ways I can best appropriate the gifts Iona has given me. I come away not only with a quieter soul but with a deeper knowledge of God's fathomless love for me and for the world.

In all its beauty and deep spiritual history, Iona is not immune to the brokenness of the world. As I mentioned earlier, monks were brutally martyred on its shores centuries ago, over many different eras. More recently, in 1998, the whole island grieved acutely when four of their young men drowned in the Sound of Iona, their small boat capsized by a rogue wave. Iona may serve as a temporary reprieve from my louder, demanding daily life, but most meaningful to me is its way of speaking into my deepest longings, my joys and my suffering, and pointing me in the direction of hope.

One of the first groups I led on pilgrimage to Iona included a colleague of mine. Gloria was a professor of education whose glowing countenance mirrored her vibrant love for God and people. She walked Iona's paths, fully engaged and eager to learn all that Iona had to teach her. As it does for so many, that pilgrimage to Iona became a marker in her life, a place where God was made known to her in profound ways.

Not long after we returned home from our pilgrimage, Gloria learned she had breast cancer. Over the next ten years or so, she resisted its power over her, obeying her doctors and prayerfully relinquishing it to God, all the while maintaining her fervor for teaching the university students she loved. When Gloria died, her husband grieved mightily. He also committed to going to Iona himself one day. He wanted to visit the sacred place that had meant so much to Gloria. So Thomas joined one of my pilgrimages, and now the isle has become his sacred place too. In important ways, Thomas brought his and Gloria's story full circle by walking those holy paths himself. He received Iona as a redemptive gift, even after such pain and loss.

When we intentionally put ourselves in a position of receptivity and attention, God will attend to us. We will find what our souls need, whether it be inspiration, or fellowship, or healing, or simply the knowledge of God's presence. This is the gift that sacred places have for us.

There is a legend on the island claiming that if you visit Iona once, you will visit three times. You will be drawn back, even if the revisiting is only possible in your memory. The sacred nature of the place, for both people of faith and those who are searching for it, is unavoidable. You will leave Iona knowing you will never be quite the same again.

To visit Iona is to recognize that we were made for another world and are dissatisfied with this one. That's not a bad thing. The discontented want something they do not yet have, and that means they are open to a breakthrough. But the key is to recognize that Iona and other sacred places have the power to break into our daily lives here and now—to teach us to find God, and shalom, in the midst of our everyday worlds, which can feel like thick places in comparison to the thin place that is Iona. The discontentment we may feel about those everyday worlds—the distance between us and the holy—can be a catalyst for change, for allowing God's spirit to meet us where we are.

QUESTIONS FOR SPIRITUAL DIRECTION

1. *Where are the sacred places in your life? How have they changed you?*
2. *If you were to be honest with God about the deepest longings of your heart, what would they be? What is keeping you from admitting them?*
3. *When have you experienced* kairos? *Is there something in your life that creates an obstacle to* kairos?

2

BOTHY

The Sacred Small

What finally matters is that our hearts become
like quiet [monastic] cells where God can dwell,
wherever we go and whatever we do.
—Henri Nouwen, *The Only Necessary Thing*

When compared to the rest of Creation, we humans
are very small. We are but a snowflake on the shoul-
der of Everest, a microscopic skin cell on the face
of the earth. And the more we learn about the universe, the more we begin to grasp just how teeny we
are. The other day, I read an article about how the
star Betelgeuse is around twelve times bigger than
our sun. I don't even know what to do with that kind
of information, except to say that it makes me feel

less self-conscious about gaining a couple of pounds over the holidays.

Is it our dinkiness that propels us to construct grand cathedrals, to make massive temples of worship so we remember how big God is? Maybe. I appreciate that sense of perspective sometimes. To sit in a pew in Westminster Abbey or Notre Dame—or at the foot of Mount Rainier, for that matter—puts me in my place. It's good to be reminded of the grandeur and the glory of God. The heavens are declaring it all the time, but sometimes it takes something huge for me to begin to comprehend it.

More than once have I sensed the nearness of God in a massive cathedral. I have especially fond memories of one Sunday when my husband Cary and I were in Germany. We were there with our friends and colleagues, Tim and Pam, sharing the leadership of a team of college students studying and touring the region that summer.

On Pentecost Sunday, we all attended the morning mass at St. Martin's church, a spectacular cathedral with a towering steeple in the middle of the charming town of Landshut. My grasp of the German language is limited to one year of study in high school, so most of the service was beyond my ability to comprehend. But one part of the service I understood with crystal clarity: as the priest read aloud from the Bible, a tiny opening in the apex of the church's ceiling revealed a niche, not more than twelve inches in diameter . . . and from it fell thousands of red and pink rose petals, floating down onto the heads and shoulders and laps of the congregation. Earlier, our friend Tim had let us in on the secret: he knew this endless shower of petals was an annual tradition in this cathedral, and he made sure our group was there to experience the illustration of what happened on that first Pentecost day. The image of the red fire of the Spirit, the scent of the holy, fell on us in a language we could all understand from a distance so high above us we might have believed God dropped those petals directly from heaven.

> I find it curious how often God shows up in relatively small places.

There is a reason that cathedrals and mountains are grand: they give us a glimpse of the transcendent grandeur of God.

I find it curious, then, how often God shows up in relatively small places. The biblical account tells us it was in a cave that Elijah learned to discern the voice of God. It was inside a fish that Jonah had his "come to Yahweh" moment. It was in his mother's womb that

John the Baptist, then just a fetus, recognized the presence of his kinsman Jesus, who was likewise in utero. And it was in a tomb that Lazarus heard the emancipating words of Christ: "Come out!"

While the early Celtic monasteries were built around a common sanctuary for worship, they also included small huts, individual "cells" just big enough for the monks to pray and sleep in. Here they could offer pastoral care to each other or to visitors. Even Columba, the abbot and founder of the monastery on Iona, lived in a cell. There he carried out his personal spiritual practices of prayer and offering spiritual direction to the monks. It is said that he slept on the cell's bare floor with a stone for a pillow. Columba knew the importance of humility in his role as spiritual father on Iona. He knew, having read about the Desert Fathers, that it is in the cell where one's soul is taught and shaped.

One summer, I chose to stay in a bothy—a shepherd's hut parked at the youth hostel on the north end of Iona. I rented it for eight days and nights, hoping to write and pray and be still before I needed to head back to Glasgow. I would meet my pilgrimage group there and return again to Iona with all of them in tow.

In Scotland, shepherds' bothies are intermittently scattered throughout the Highlands. These bare-bones huts are left unlocked and open for hikers to use for shelter. If you should find yourself hiking through the Highlands and need a place to stay, keep an eye out for a bothy. You might discover one that is already occupied by other hikers, but the unofficial bothy protocol requires the sharing of space with strangers. If you have your own bedding, some food, and a few stories to share around the fire, it might all add up to a jolly evening with new friends.

I'm not usually open to such a prospect. Staying in a bothy sounds entirely too similar to *camping*, which I've only done once in my life (thank you, high school youth group). The Ozarks of northwest Arkansas, where we make our home, are a haven for campers. Even so, I happily leave that sort of adventuring to my kids and their families, while Cary and I check into the nearest bed-and-breakfast.

For whatever reason, that particular summer I had the urge to ditch my usual attachment to the Argyll Hotel and opted for the "wee bothy." My family was stunned to hear that I was considering accommodations that had no indoor plumbing. It is true enough that the hut contained no running water, no toilet. But the youth hostel just down the path had facilities to use, and I could manage that fine. It was a price I was willing to pay for a week of solitude and silence, for a cell of my own.

What the bothy did have was charm. Constructed of blue metal siding with a gray corrugated roof, it sat on wheels like a Romani caravan at the foot of Iona's solitary mountain, called Dun I ("dun-ee"). The bothy's windows opened to the sea, revealing an uninterrupted view of the islands of Tiree and Coll and the quirky little blink of an island called the Dutchman's Cap. Inside, the walls were painted a clean ivory, and the windows were appropriately dressed in tartan plaid curtains. A comfy bed, a small turquoise table and chair, and a small hutch near the door assured me that this shepherd's hut was significantly nicer than those that are free to hikers in the Highlands. One final element confirmed that suspicion: electricity. This would be critical for the British traveler; how else would one heat water for tea? There was an electric kettle, fresh bottled water, and a healthy selection of teas, sugar, and tiny pods of milk (I love the nonrefrigerated option that's available in the UK).

For eight days and nights, the cozy shed looking out to the Atlantic was my home, my days at once simple and luxurious. No frills except for the exquisite Iona-scape of land and sea. No schedule except for the simple rhythm I had created for myself each day. And absolutely no fear. I felt completely safe out there by myself without a phone, in the middle of nowhere. (The animals on Iona are completely non-threatening, unless you happen to stumble into the path of one of the Highland bulls that tend to hang about on the farmland on the island's midsection.) Outside the bothy sat a bench, providing a perfect place for sitting and writing in the sun, a spot I took advantage of regularly.

Even the need to use the bathroom in the middle of the night proved to have its own share of delight: since summertime brings daylight at four in the morning, I witnessed a sunrise or two and some wet bunny tracks on the stepping-stones. With those glimpses arose the simple joy of feeling that in this space and time, I was the only one witnessing this beauty. The bothy offered me silence and solitude. I can't think of a more satisfying experience than to occupy a space that was "mine," for a time that was completely my own, with no source of disruption or distraction. Some might see this as self-indulgent. But anyone who notices the night sky, a little gathering of trees in a local city park, or the moment when all that has been noise goes very still will know this: silence, space, and security in God's presence are essential for the health of a soul.

My time in the bothy confirmed the wisdom of Jesus, in his teaching that we ought to go into our closet to pray. We may find that a grand European cathedral is an inspiring place to be in awe of God. And on the other end of the spectrum, we might find one of our sacred spaces is the closet. The soul craves a secret place, unseen by a world that seeks to be impressive. A place where conversations can be had with God in ways that a bustling church building may not afford.

At my home in Arkansas, economy and space have allowed us to have a bit of land, about an acre and a half. Our modest home sits right in the middle. When the trees in the backyard lose their leaves each fall, we can literally see Oklahoma, so you could say ours is the last house in Arkansas.

The back corner of our yard has tempted me for years with its possibilities. With the Oklahoma countryside and farmland immediately behind it, it is a perfect place (in my estimation) for a small hut . . . a space where I imagine my own bothy, my own cell. A place for writing, for meeting with people coming for spiritual direction, for silence, for prayer. I can spend a good bit of time imagining how to make such a place happen.

Perhaps that time would be more fruitfully spent working with what I've already got. Where are the small spaces that are available to me that I might consecrate as my own "cell"? Author Cindy Bunch recommends the spiritual practice of creating a home altar, a designated area in the home where we can arrange visual objects to draw our attention to God and what God is saying. She suggests beginning with a small shelf or bench; her own home altar sits under a window next to a chair in her home where she regularly sits for prayer. She then selects from various items in a collection she keeps nearby and accessible—colorful cloth, a cross, candles, mementos, pebbles, cards, photos, a Bible. The altar can be arranged to reflect a season of the church year, like using a red cloth during the season of Pentecost, or simply to mark the season of life we are in.

I love the idea of a home altar because it can be very personal. Each item is a physical expression of what we are offering to God in faith, trusting him to care and provide for the concerns we carry. The objects on our altars can also remind us of who God is, particularly if they help us recall the ways God has cared for us in the past or the truths he has spoken into our lives.

> I love the idea of a home altar because it can be very personal. Each item is a physical expression of what we are offering to God in faith.

When we hear the word *altar*, we might typically imagine something imposing, like an altar in a cathedral. I immediately think of the great altar in Iona Abbey, beautifully carved out of the white-and-green marble found at the south end of the island. I love that altar because it represents the splendor of God, but altars don't have to be stately in order to establish a pocket of holiness. Bunch's idea of a home altar is a small but important means of connecting with God. Perhaps I will lay dried rose petals from the church in Germany on my altar, reminding me that God is near and accessible in the person of the Holy Spirit. Maybe I will place one of the miniature ceramic bothies I've brought home from Iona, reminding me of the ways God has been my shelter and protector.

Through the years, my Bible has also served as a type of altar. So many significant events in life naturally come accompanied by some manner of printed material to help mark them—a ticket stub, a program, a handwritten note. These are the same kinds of things that could be placed on a home altar; mine somehow find their way into my Bible. You can't turn many pages in it before encountering a Benedictine prayer card, a train ticket for one of my group pilgrimages, a postcard of my favorite painting sent from my daughter in London, or a bookmark that belonged to my grandmother. When I come to God in the pages of my Bible, these small altar items remind me that I bring God my whole life. Simultaneously they remind me to give thanks for God's generous gifts to me.

Iona Abbey is quite a sight, especially as you approach it on the village road. The grand structure is the result of a restoration effort that began in 1874 and continued in fits and starts until its completion in 1965. It's important to keep in mind that the abbey we see today was not Columba's. His monastery's church would have been made of primitive materials like mud, wattle, and thatch. The current abbey is the restored worship center that originally served a Benedictine community on Iona in the early 1200s. The Columban community had long since dissipated by then, but the Benedictine Abbey was constructed in its exact place.

Just to the left of the entrance to the abbey grounds stands Tòrr an Aba, the Hill of the Abbot. This hill is believed to be the location of Columba's writing hut, also known as a cell or a scriptorium. The location is significant because, according to Adomnán, Columba's biographer, this is where Columba spent many days and nights—praying, sleeping, copying scriptures, and providing guidance to the monks in his care.

In the summer of 2017, I caught sight of an article announcing a discovery of archaeological significance on Iona confirmed by such sources as the BBC and the University of Glasgow. Apparently, Tòrr an Aba was excavated back in 1957 with noted British archaeologist Charles Thomas at the helm. His team found what appeared to be the remains of a wattle hut—a small enclosure made of woven sticks and twigs. The remains had been intentionally covered with pebbles from the beach, and at the mound's summit was a hole where a stone or wood cross would likely have stood. Everything pointed to the discovery of Columba's hut, but the sophisticated process of radiocarbon dating was not as accessible in the fifties as it is now. The cost at that time was too great and the results would not have been reliable, so decades passed, and Charles Thomas kept his carefully preserved samples unceremoniously tucked away in his garage.

Fast-forward to the twenty-first century, when archaeologists from the University of Glasgow somehow heard about the samples. With the happy cooperation of Charles Thomas and funding from Historic Environment Scotland, and with support from the National Trust for Scotland, the now more advanced process of radiocarbon dating was applied to the samples found on Tòrr an Aba. The results were exactly what everyone had hoped: the excavated samples were dated between 540 and 650 CE; Columba died in 597. The location of Columba's scriptorium was no longer an educated guess but a scientific fact.

With the proof that St. Columba, abbot of Iona, lived and prayed and counseled there on the Hill of the Abbot, an enhanced appreciation for his life emerges for me. I like to freely imagine him standing on that very hill, next to his hut, a tall cross erected there to mark it as a holy place. I picture him looking out over the faith community as the monks performed their daily rounds—working in the dairy barn, feeding sheep, going to prayer. I imagine him worry-praying that the monks would be able to stand up to the challenges that came their way from within and without, that the winter would be kind so that illness and death would not snatch some of them away, and that he would be granted spiritual wisdom to lead his community in ministry beyond their island's shores.

As I stand on the Hill of the Abbot, I am given the image of Columba—a small man, in a small hut, leading a small community, on a small island. From a tiny spot on the globe, Columba began what would become a colossal movement of Christian spiritual vitality. Columba's life illustrates that we humans are small indeed. Perhaps it makes sense that our small ears can hear the voice of God better in a small place, like a cave, or a bothy, or the silence of our own souls.

We too easily minimize the good that can be done by seemingly insignificant people in inconsequential places. Ours is a world where influence is measured by the number of likes or followers on social media. For every fantastic story that goes viral, there are countless others that are never told—stories about faithful people aware of their smallness in obscure or forgotten places who bless the world. History reminds us that those "small" stories matter, more than we may ever know.

I have my own small role to play, and so do you.

If we hope to find out what it is, spending some time in our cell is a start.

It will teach us everything.

QUESTIONS FOR SPIRITUAL DIRECTION

1. *Where do you go to meet with God? Why does that place have meaning for you?*

2. *Who are the "small" people in your life who have led you to great spiritual insights?*

3

STAFFA

Wonder

See your imagination dawn
Around the rim of your world.
—John O'Donohue, *To Bless the Space Between Us*

We boarded the *Iolaire* with wobbly legs and eager anticipation. The captain offered his hand to steady each of us as we stepped gingerly from the jetty onto the bobbing deck.

Each time I lead our weeklong pilgrimage to Iona, I offer my group an afternoon excursion off-island, and this was that day. While Iona is unusual in its distinction as a thin place, a sacred place, it is but one tiny island in a collection of nearly eighty islands off the western coast of Scotland. The island we were destined for that day is Staffa—uninhabited and known for its dramatic basalt columns that stretch upward out of the sea. Felix Mendelssohn's famous *Hebrides* overture was inspired by Fingal's Cave, a great cavern carved out of the base of Staffa, the result of determined waves pounding against rock for untold millennia.

The *Iolaire*—Gaelic for "eagle" and pronounced "eye-oh-lare"—is not a large boat. My group obediently lined up at the jetty early that afternoon in order to secure seats at the front in the open air. It's worth it; it can be a wild ride as the *Iolaire* speeds along toward Staffa, rocking dramatically with the force of the current. Even in summer months, a wool stocking cap is a necessity against the chilly wind. Another requirement for me are anti–motion sickness meds; experience has taught me the cost of forgetting them.

On this trip to Staffa, we were welcomed aboard the *Iolaire* by a young man who was, I'm guessing, twelve or thirteen years old. I will call him Ben (though anyone living on Iona would easily recognize him, I'm sure). He was assisting on the boat during the summer tourist season, and it wasn't long before we saw that he took this role very seriously. Our boat had hardly left the Iona jetty when Ben made his precocious presence known, greeting each passenger, asking them where they were from, and dutifully recording their answers on a legal pad. He seemed especially pleased to announce that there were only two states in the United States that had not been present on one of their trips that summer.

In his pronounced Scottish accent, Ben made us all aware of safety precautions while on the boat. He returned to his easy charm, working the crowd. He drew our attention to the seals lazing on the warm pink stone of the Isle of Mull to our right as we sailed through the Sound of Iona; the islands of Tiree and Coll were off to the west as we emerged into open sea.

Our boat bumped along, dramatically responding to the rhythm of the waves. The wind was cold and fierce. The volume of the boat engine and the natural sounds of the wind and waves competed against each other. We huddled close as Ben asked how we were liking Scotland so far. He seemed genuinely pleased with our enthusiastic responses. In turn, we asked him what it was like growing up on Iona. Did he ever wish he lived somewhere else—a place that offered more amusements, more opportunities, more . . . people? His response was genuine: "No, no, I love living on Iona! It has been the best place for me to grow up."

Ben drew our attention to the seabirds that flew around us as we sailed, easily identifying them:

gannets, kittiwakes, razorbills. Then he steered the conversation to a topic that was clearly his favorite and his area of expertise: *puffins*.

This pleased me to no end. Seeing the puffins on Staffa is my supreme goal for my group and the reason I schedule my pilgrimages for midsummer. Only during the summer months does the colony come onto the island to dig burrows and lay their eggs. Ben shared his knowledge of puffins with glee, his eager audience in the palm of his hand.

He talked to us about the life span of puffins (twenty years or more), their burrows and how many eggs they lay each summer (just one), what they eat (small herring-like fish called sand eels), and how they feel safe and secure when humans are around because apparently we keep the gulls away. I have since learned that black gulls are their natural predator and that they can snatch a puffin in midair. The puffin's scientific name, *Fratercula arctica*, means "little brother of the north," alluding to the puffin's black-and-white plumage—squat little birds dressed up like monks. Similarly amusing are the terms for a group of puffins, including "a colony, a puffinry, a circus, a burrow, a gathering, or an improbability."

I like to think that puffins are animals God created just for the sheer fun of it.

Soon enough, the *Iolaire* approached the imposing island of Staffa. It is a great rock of an island, wrapped in towering hexagonal basalt columns that make it look like something out of The Lord of the Rings. The orderly composition of the columns suggests that Staffa was constructed, not created, but that's not the case. Geologists know that millions of years ago, the lava that flowed from a volcano on nearby Mull emerged from the sea. Staffa, in all its magnificence, was the result.

Our boat docked at the small pier, and our lips tasted sea salt. The captain used the loudspeaker to remind us that we had just sixty minutes to spend on Staffa and had two choices: either head straight up the hill to see the puffins or take a hard left and walk around the lower edge of the island to see the famous Fingal's Cave. I had seen Fingal's Cave, and it is indeed impressive. Scotland's National Trust has installed a good handrail that hugs the hulking edge of the island, making an otherwise uneven pathway to the cave passable. The cave is a phenomenal sight, and the acoustics are remarkable. My group may have sung "How Great Thou Art" there a time or two.

But if I must choose, I will take the puffins over the cave every time. If you and I could sit down in a coffee shop and you were somehow inspired to ask me about Staffa, there is no question that I would yammer on about puffins. To sit in the tufty grass atop of Staffa with a 360-degree view of the Atlantic and the Hebridean isles is thrilling enough. Add to that an up-close encounter with these comical winged creatures and the result is an experience that brings pure joy. Be assured that as you sipped your latte of choice, I would pull out the photo album stored on my phone, and you would be subject to some of the most colorful, whimsical images you've ever seen. I guarantee, you would be grinning by the end.

The captain assisted us once again, and we each stepped off the boat onto the pier. After many journeys, I know the way across Staffa quite well. But I was so captivated by Ben's knowledge of puffins specifically, and the island in general, that I was happy to let him lead us. We followed him up the steep stairway (and by steep I mean, *hang on to the handrail and don't look down*), ascending 138 feet up to the top of the cliff. Winded and exhilarated, we began our trek across the top of Staffa.

After a short hike, we arrived at the perfect spot for encountering the puffins. The colors of the landscape were intense: the clover green of the thick, ferny grass, sloping precipitously downward to jagged charcoal-gray rocks, the indigo sea rounding out a palette of pleasing and soothing colors. I did my best not to wonder whether anyone had ever slipped; what a tragic tumble that would be. And yet there we were, sitting on the edge of the world, waiting for birds.

We silently waited, not wanting to give the wee birds any reason not to come visit. But we didn't have to wait long. Some arrived in the expected way—flying in, wobbling like drunken airmen, their orange-footed landing gear splayed out ahead of them and landing at our feet. Others caught us completely by surprise, suddenly popping out of their burrows, dug into the ground right next to where we'd been sitting. They waddled around us like clowny little ducks, not a care in the world.

Their carefree antics drew us into the spectacle of their surroundings of sea and sky, cleansing wind, and thick tufts of grass and woolly bog cotton sprouting at our feet. The puffins were not afraid of us, mingling easily as they went about their business. Oh, to know such hospitality, such confidence! That, like a puffin, I could so easily welcome strangers to my habitat and urge them to sit a spell—that I could be so free of any preoccupation with landing well or walking gracefully.

I sat in wonder on that great rock of Staffa, baffled at how a tiny, comical bird could so deftly deliver lessons from the Creator.

In the Bible, we read about some pretty spectacular revelations of God to his people: pillars of fire and cloud that led the children of Israel through the wilderness, the holy presence of men who survived a fiery furnace, and the most profound of all, the incarnation of Jesus—fully God, fully man, fully present and walking around Palestine.

Some of us nowadays wonder aloud why God no longer makes himself known in such obvious ways. Even if we're devout, we meet days of bleary confusion when the Jesus we follow seems to have stealthily taken off in a different direction, leaving no concrete evidence of his presence.

This is when a good spiritual director will gently clear our vision, helping us revisit moments of wonder and experience the Divine presence again. We don't have to be on a remote island surrounded by whimsical creatures to be in the presence of things wondrous. The bigger challenge in our sensory-saturated world is to give those experiences more attention, following their lead to the wonder and the truths God wants us to receive.

Iona has pointed me to God through many experiences that are grand and wondrous. But it has also revealed God to me in rather ordinary ways there as well: my serendipitous encounter with Jann, an islander who has helped me with my pilgrimages in the past and the wonder of meeting her new baby son; the deep comfort of a hot cup of tea after hiking against a wicked, chilling wind on the north shore; the stirring effect of Scripture read aloud in the abbey, its words echoing off of the ancient walls; the wonder of young Ben and his enthusiasm for his island home.

Whenever I return home from Iona, I'm determined to grow in appreciating the wonder that is in my life—whether it be spectacular or rather ordinary. Because this is really the point of it all. Iona may be my spiritual home, but it is not my earthly home; if I'm lucky, I am there once a year for a week or so. The rest of the time I live and work and write and play in the northwest corner of Arkansas, a place

> We don't have to be on a remote island surrounded by whimsical creatures to be in the presence of things wondrous.

that most people would assume to be completely unremarkable.

And they would be wrong.

In my little town, there is every bit as much wonder to behold as on the mighty Isle of Staffa. God shows up with regularity if I have eyes to see, if I condition myself to be attentive to the colorful, multidimensional work of God around me that is no less amazing than a comical puffin bringing sand eels to its burrow.

As I've mentioned, we have a big Southern porch (something you don't find on Iona) that faces east and is a marvelous spot for watching birds and other wildlife. The other day I sat there with our dog, Rory, drinking in the peace of a day off work and enjoying the mild temperatures of the season. Without warning, two deer bolted across our front yard and into the woods across the street, white tails standing at attention. Watching them bound so gracefully across our front lawn reminded me that the wonders of God can surprise us at any moment. What made it truly extraordinary, however, was that I had time to relish the experience afterward, to let the encounter sink in and remind me of the beauty that accompanies all work of God. Rory and I just looked at each other: *Wow, what was that?* My soul grows stronger when I take the time to answer that question: *It was a gift, that's what it was.* A thing of beauty placed in front of me. An expression of God's love.

In my work, I'm privileged to see university students bolt across the campus and out into the world. They come to us as freshmen, appropriately clueless about what life holds for them. But come commencement day, four (or so) years later, they have been shaped into people who, if we've done our work right, are equipped to think critically and make contributions to the world that have eternal consequences. Like the deer coming out of nowhere, their transformation is stunning. When I hear them testify of the ways they have been challenged to become the people God is calling them to be, I am filled with wonder. How does this happen, this incredible example of the artistry of God?

> Wherever we may find ourselves, there is spectacle to behold, drawing our attention to what is numinous, transcendent.

In a world that is desperate for hope, it is up to us to celebrate the grandeur of God and God's work, both visible and invisible. Wherever we may find ourselves, there is spectacle to behold, drawing our attention to what is numinous, transcendent. It is another way the Holy Spirit incites "home" in us, drawing us to what is holy and increasing our longing for Creation as it was meant to be.

Our extended family—fifteen of us, cousins included—love to gather at my in-laws' lakeside home here in the Ozarks. The youngest member, our four-year-old granddaughter, Lizzy Iona, learned from her earliest days that watching birds is a big deal in the Balzer clan, a source of true wonder.

In the course of a weekend together, one or more of us will be standing on the glassed-in porch, high among the trees, watching the broad variety of birds that visit the lakehouse. Lizzy has learned that this is what we do. And when we see a great blue heron or a pileated woodpecker, we exclaim with Ben-like enthusiasm and do everything we can to help little Lizzy see the birds.

One morning when she was just a toddler, Lizzy came to me in the lakehouse kitchen, still in her kitty-print pajamas, and said, "Go watch birds?" I complied, of course. We had just casually walked out to the porch when a bald eagle swooped into our view, cruising above the lake and continuing down to the other end of the cove. I instinctively called out to any family members within earshot, "Bald eagle bald eagle bald eagle!" It vanished as quickly as it had arrived. But what a spectacle it was, its bright white head and tail in sharp contrast to the leafless trees beyond, declaring that it was indeed winter—the season for bald trees and bald eagles.

Lizzy, satisfied that her request to see birds had been spectacularly fulfilled, ran through the house exclaiming with glee, "I saw a bald eagle! White head!" We were all delighted to share her excitement. The newest member of our tribe had just unwittingly passed a rite of initiation without any prodding or provoking. She had learned it quite naturally from being around us, her bird-loving family.

If we want to grow in wonder, one of the most effective ways is to glean the ability from someone else. There's a fine line between a person whose enthusiasm is contagious and someone whose zeal is obnoxious or smothering. The first kind can be a teacher in our quest for wonder. So before we go hunting for wonder-full experiences, perhaps we should seek after someone who really knows how to do it, who can point us in the right direction toward the wonder that is life-giving.

Do you know someone who is excited about astronomy? Ask them to show you their telescope and introduce you to the cosmos in a way you've not experienced before. One late night years ago, we took our young girls to a wooded state park not far from our town. The local astronomy club had invited anyone interested to come join them for their monthly stargazing event. We have always been fascinated by anything related to space and were eager for our daughters to see beyond what our inexpensive family telescope could show them. Our hosts were almost giddy that guests had come, and after regaling us with their knowledge about what we were going to see, they led us to the great telescope. The planet Saturn! Wonder! It was astonishing to view an object otherwise invisible to our eyes, like seeing a wiggling paramecium under a microscope for the first time.

But it wasn't only the viewing that got us excited; it was being with people who were genuinely enthusiastic about the heavens declaring "the glory of God" like the Psalm writer said (Psalm 19:1). I've never looked at the night sky in the same way since. Those enthusiastic stargazers passed their wonderment on to us.

Listening to anyone who is an expert in something always incites wonder in me. Their topic doesn't have to be something I particularly care about or have been wondering about. But if I listen to them and learn why their expertise fills them with wonder, I invariably leave that lecture or conference or demonstration with a newfound interest and appreciation for their subject. I suspect that this is one of the reasons TED talks are so compelling. We can listen to a person talk about their passion for (fill in the blank) for twenty minutes and come away shaking our heads and saying, "I never knew that!"

Wonder is contagious. It can be passed on from teacher to student, from grandfather to granddaughter, from Ben to a group of foreigners surrounded by puffins. This kind of wonder can be the story of our lives as we actively seek occasions to celebrate the wondrous works of God in Creation. And it can begin with learning from God's finest creations: each other.

Prepare to be amazed.

QUESTIONS FOR SPIRITUAL DIRECTION

1. *Where have you experienced true wonder in your own life? Where have you experienced it in your travels?*

2. *How has that wonder been infused into your awareness of God?*

3. *What are some ways you might share that wonder with others in your life?*

4. *Is there a part of creation that you've been curious about but haven't found a way to explore? What might you do to make that happen?*

4

BRIGHT MOMENTS

The Breath of God

Blessed are they who see beautiful things in humble places where others see nothing.

—Camille Pissarro

When I was pregnant with our first daughter, I discovered a little magic trick. I learned that if I took in a deep breath, the baby would receive a flush of oxygen—and would respond with a healthy wiggle or kick. It was a gratifying game for me (even if my ribs took a bit of a beating), for it assured me that all was well in there. I'd like to think it gave my tiny daughter a bit of excitement as well, a surge of energy that offered her a taste of the thrill of life, a reason to look forward to joining us on the outside. Oh, the adventures we would have.

In a similar way, I discover God will sometimes "breathe" in my direction, which energizes and revitalizes my spirit in a way that is both refreshing and inspiring. My faith isn't dependent on these periodic bursts of spiritual oxygen, but when they come, I receive them as gifts. I try to keep a record of them in my journal and review them periodically. They serve as a sort of charm bracelet, adorned with all the bright moments that God has used to carry me through each season of life.

In Kenneth Steven's captivating novel *The Well of the North Wind*, I came across the phrase "God of the bright moments." It has never left me. I found the book at the Waterstones bookshop in Oban, the seaside town that serves as a transfer point between train and ferry on the journey to and from Iona. Best known as a poet, Kenneth's prolific work artistically illustrates Hebridean life, particularly on Iona, with expert skill and grace. His poetry has accompanied my own Iona journeys for years. When I saw his new novel, set in the time of Columba and adorned with a stunning cover of blue and green brushstrokes, I knew I would love it. The "signed by author" sticker sealed the deal, and soon enough it was with me on the train back to Glasgow.

I devoured that book. It satisfied my hunger for the things I have come to love about Iona: the sea, the landscape, its monastic history, the sacredness of it all. I felt compelled to express my gratitude to its author. On a whim, I found his website and left him a note of appreciation.

Several months later, my office phone rang. "Hello," said a kind voice on the other end, "this is Kenneth Steven calling." Thoroughly bewildered but (unfortunately) not speechless, I blurted out, "Why are you calling me?" Despite my unclassy response, Kenneth remained on the line, apologetically explaining that his website had gotten mucked up, preventing him from accessing any comments from readers that were left there. Rather than reply electronically to the note I'd left about his book, he decided to give me a call.

I don't know about you, but for me, the discovery of a true kindred spirit is one of life's most gratifying experiences. On the phone that day, Kenneth and I—he in Scotland, I in the States—enjoyed our shared faith, our mutual love of Iona and the Celtic story, our passion for writing. That bright moment of collegiality has turned into a friendship that has breathed encouragement and inspiration into me in ways I could not have predicted.

The downstairs lounge at the Argyll Hotel on Iona is the very picture of Scottish charm and warmth. All the essential elements are there: a fireplace stoked with peat bricks (if you haven't encountered the earthy scent of a good peat fire, put it on your bucket list), walls of ancient stone, comfy couches, coffee and tea easily acquired from the fine Argyll staff, and the most important component—a view of the sea. When I add my personal essentials— a pen and journal—I am in a perfect state of contentment.

One morning, I sat in that lounge with each of these variables in place, completely alone, drinking in the quiet and settling in for an unhurried time of peaceful contemplation. I could see the Sound of Iona through the window as its gentle waves rolled from south to north. Islanders walked past now and then, smiling dogs at the end of their leads. The entrance to the hotel is just outside the door of the lounge, so I could hear folk coming and going. I smiled to think of any first-time visitors walking into this welcoming place, knowing the gift that was in store for them.

My peaceful pondering was suddenly interrupted as the door of the lounge opened and a gentleman's head popped in.

"Please come in," I responded, not wanting to presume command over the whole lounge. Suddenly, a moment of recognition descended: it was Alan, whom I had met two years before when we were members of a group retreat at the Argyll. He did indeed come in, and after a cheerful moment of reunion, he took a seat on the sofa across from me.

Alan is a delightful Scottish soul, full of light and genuine kindness. We had spent only a few days together on that retreat two years before, but you'd think I was his long-lost sister, so warm and enthusiastic was his greeting, so eager was his inquiry into my life. Alan had recently gotten married—right there on Iona, in fact— so I was keen to hear all his news as well. He and his bride had married in a small ceremony at the Bishop's House, a chapel and retreat center that sits just above the Sound of Iona. Their wedding reception was held afterward at the Argyll. I experienced his joy as he showed me photos on his phone of the happy day.

We were furiously chatting away when suddenly, Alan's good friend Peter popped his head in. Peter was also at our retreat two years ago and, like Alan, had returned for another. It took only seconds for me to be reminded of how fascinating Peter is, a scholar and historian from Liverpool, full of enthusiasm for nature and stories of the Hebridean isles. Combine the distinctive accent of George Harrison or Ringo Starr with a scholar's knowledge of Scotland, and you'll have Peter. (I have a vague memory of Peter once relating an anecdote about going to school with one or more of the Beatles, but that's his story to tell, not mine.) The conversation quickly grew more vigorous as the three of us moved from pleasantries to our shared love for Iona as a place of holy beauty. I couldn't believe my good fortune: another joyful reunion punctuating the presence of a bright moment.

Before long, two more joined our group in the lounge; Dee and Jan had also been part of the retreat two years ago. Serendipity! (And coming from an introvert like me, this is saying something.)

Alan ordered coffee for all of us. There we were, five people, all from different places in the world, enjoying the gift of this unexpected reunion. The brightness of the moment was solidified by the fellowship of kindred souls, fortuitously brought together for a cup of coffee on a remote pinpoint of an island.

The world roils around us, with so many examples of damaged relationships, shady leadership, and an abused environment. But in a stony lounge by the sea, my soul over-flowed with gratitude. The bright moments of life remind me how deeply I am *known* by God and how deeply I am *loved* by God, even treasured. When I encounter a stunning book or a fascinating person or a place that stirs my soul and brings tears to my eyes, I sit up and pay attention. Such moments shine a spotlight on the fact that I am created uniquely by God and help me better discern where to find God. As C. S. Lewis put it, "These pure and spontaneous pleasures are 'patches of Godlight' in the woods of our experience."

The bright moments of my life also draw me out of my introverted shell, for nearly every time God has sent a bright moment my way, it is not for me alone; others are part of the scheme. People, fellow-ship, connection—God seems to be quite keen on "matchmaking," on bringing us together.

Romantics speak of the "spark" that happens when two people first meet and find something

The bright moments of life remind me how deeply I am *known* by God and how deeply I am *loved* by God, even treasured.

irresistibly attractive in each other. That "spark" didn't exist until these two met, but within just a few moments or hours, something definitely catches fire. I have witnessed this phenomenon firsthand. When our daughter returned home one night from a New Year's Eve party, she was glowing; she had met a guy named Jake. They were married a year and a half later.

Similarly, when believers and spiritual seekers come together, there is the potential for light, warmth, and transformation. The brightest moments of my life have, in one way or another, connected me to the body of Christ. The phone call from Kenneth and that simple reunion in the lounge are both examples of bright moments. The personal transformation that began then continues to this day, as it should. I am a different person because of them.

To soak up these bright moments, these "patches of Godlight," is not to deny the brokenness of the world. Rather, they spur us on to be healers and survivors when the grayer clouds are threatening. God is a redeemer, and so of course God is also the one who comforts and sustains in the midst of trial.

Bleak moments are real, even bleak seasons. These are times when all those lovely, soul-stirring experiences seem to be nothing but a dream, a superficial encounter with real faith, and cynicism threatens to take hold. When bleakness threatens, I need more than a bright moment; I need a bright *presence*.

When anxiety threatens to overwhelm, the only prayer I can pray is the one that has been carved on my heart over years of trying to follow Jesus: "Lord Jesus Christ, son of God, have mercy on me, a sinner." This is known as the Jesus Prayer, and it's been recited for centuries by people in the Eastern Orthodox tradition of Christianity. I'm not Eastern Orthodox, but to me this prayer is a lifesaver, thrown to me when I feel I am drowning. The fact that it has given comfort to so many people for so many years assures me I am in good company. It's a prayer that gives me words when my innermost being cannot possibly articulate the state of my soul. The prayer has its origins in a Gospel story, uttered by two blind men who were desperate for healing and shouted out to Jesus, "Lord, Son of David, have mercy on us!" (Matthew 20:30) The people around them, rather than having compassion, told them to shut up.

I know what it's like to want to be healed. Each of us longs for healing in a particular way. But what I especially identify with is how these men must have felt when the crowd rebuked them. A similar crowd populates my head, routinely scolding me for being so needy. When the bleak moments come, my soul's enemy loves to taunt and shame me for feeling sorry for myself, especially because there are countless people who know true suffering in this world. I get hit by both sides—by the circumstances that have instigated the bleak moment and by the voice of shame and guilt that scolds me for not being able to manage it better. It can leave me gasping for breath, my spiritual oxygen levels rapidly declining.

This is when Jesus enters in. In the Gospel story, Jesus doesn't continue on his way, ignore their petition, or tell them other people have it far worse so they should stop complaining. He stops and asks, "What do you want me to do for you?" And then he touches their eyes and heals their blindness.

In my bleakest times, I am one of the blind men on the road, lost in darkness, be it emotional, physical, or spiritual. But the God of the bright moments is always walking in my direction. God knows what I need but asks anyway: *What do you want me to do for you?* At God's word, God's breath, the curtains of my darkness begin to part. Light comes in. The bleak moment (or day, or year) passes, and I can see again.

Jesus knows, experientially, what it is like to live in a bleak world and how desperately we all need the bright moment of his healing presence.

To hear Jesus ask me "What do you want me to do for you?" is a deeply healing experience, for I become aware not only that Jesus *can* help me but that he *intends* to. In my desire to know and experience God, it is important for me to believe that in the same way, I am heard and seen and cared for.

It's tempting to dismiss these bright moments as merely flashes of serendipity, of coincidence. I contend that they are limited only by our response to them. We've already considered that hallowed moments are often found in small things and small places and that God does not have a habit of appearing to us in spectacular ways. Rather, we note God's presence when we take time to observe the humble, everyday miracles and, now and then, the bright moments. These will not make the newspapers, but they should surely hold space in our private journals.

Where wonder requires attention, bright moments demand reflection. When we take the time to carefully ponder our bright moments, we begin to perceive that they're not merely serendipitous events or happy coincidences. There are patterns at work. Meaningful reflection requires that we take the time not only to wonder at what is before us but to ask two questions: *Why* was this moment so meaningful to me? And *how* am I to respond to this meaning? Raising those questions reveals how a particular moment helps us receive the love God has for us and how our lives might be different as a result.

> Bright moments demand reflection. When we take the time to carefully ponder our bright moments, we begin to perceive that they're not merely serendipitous events or happy coincidences. There are patterns at work.

I have experienced unexpected reunions before, when old friends suddenly find each other in the same place at the same time, passing each other at an airport or eating at the same restaurant. Why was the reunion at the Argyll so especially meaningful to me? What made it a "bright moment" while similar situations were merely happy accidents?

My journal serves a vital role here, because I don't readily know how to answer that question until I've reflected upon it. As I write out my mostly random and eventually more cogent thoughts, the fog begins to lift. I begin to recognize the personal ways that an experience has touched me, like the way Alan and Peter clearly communicated that my presence, my thoughts, and my shared love for Iona were of great value to them. They seemed genuinely delighted to see me and revel in our peculiar and commonly held interest. Likewise, their deep knowledge of that transcendent place knit us together in a palpable way. It was an easy and enthusiastic conversation that I sometimes find curiously difficult to replicate in my own hometown.

My journal then helps me with the next step that educators love to refer to as the "practical application": How does this experience change me? I gradually realize that my own way of communicating with others could use an upgrade. Genuine, kind attention to others, including the leisurely pace set by partaking of tea or coffee, happens often enough on a planned basis, confirmed by the success of coffee shops all over our country. But I'm chagrined to say that I rarely allow a spontaneous, unplanned gathering to interrupt my day. In fact, moments of spontaneous, leisurely conversation can make me downright grumpy if they are not previously scheduled on my calendar.

Yet I know that spontaneous interruptions can be startling gifts. I walked into my office the other day to find a brown package that had arrived for me. When a package's shape and weight hint that there may be a book inside, well, it's already a bright moment. But when the postmark is marked Royal Mail, my heart leaps: *Who in the UK has sent something to me?* It's the same combination of disbelief and delight that I felt when Kenneth first called me on the phone.

I tore into that package like a child on Christmas morning and indeed found a book about the Hebrides—*Folksongs and Folklore of South Uist* by Margaret Fay Shaw. Inside its cover was a letter with a return address that included the name of a cottage—a touch of British charm. It was from Alan, my kind friend with whom I was reunited in the Argyll lounge. He was thoughtfully following up on our meeting, eager to nurture my enthusiasm for the Hebrides. The book was one he had cited in our conversation, and he knew I would appreciate it. With small tears of gratitude, I promptly replied with an email confirming that I did.

It was yet another opportunity to reflect upon a bright moment.

QUESTIONS FOR SPIRITUAL DIRECTION

1. *What are some "bright moments" you have experienced lately, and why have they been meaningful?*
2. *What do you do when you are in the midst of a "bleak moment" and you're not sure how to reach out for God?*
3. *As he asked the blind men, if Jesus were to ask you what you wanted him to do for you, how would you reply?*

II
WHO AM I?

5

TUMBLING

Polishing the Soul

Conversion means starting with who we are, not
who we wish we were.

—Kathleen Norris, *Dakota*

A small glass bowl sits on my desk in my home office.
It is filled with smooth stones—some quite small,
others the size of a robin's egg. I've learned the geolog-
ical names of the three different kinds of stones in the
bowl: glassy green serpentine, white-and green-speck-
led Iona marble, and deep olive-green epidote. They
are a simple treasure, all nestled together in the bowl
with their shared green theme. I have taught my
granddaughter to hold one to her cheek, to feel the
satisfying coolness of its glassy surface.

Each of these stones has been tossed up onto the beach at Columba's Bay at the southern end of Iona, having been through a fierce tumbling process. Far beneath the visible surface of the ocean's tumult, the stones are vigorously tossed about, over and over, until the waves throw them onto the sand, where their smoothly polished surfaces are revealed.

How long does it take to make a rough stone smooth? Decades? Centuries? Millennia? It has been said that to hold a stone of Iona in your hand is to hold the history of the world. All I know is that the result is beautiful to behold.

I feel a curious kinship with those stones; I recognize that tumbling process. It comes with being human. From the mightiest to the weakest, each of us is vulnerable to the great tension and friction that is part of this temporal life on earth. Before Jesus went through his own harsh tumbling, the victim of a cruel and unjust execution on a cross, he told his friends straight up: *You are going to have trouble in this world.* Trouble. Tumbling.

Yes, he was certainly right about that.

Whether it comes in the form of an evil disease, unexpected unemployment, injustice and cruelty, or the loss of someone dear, we know that trouble. We have been given the gift of life in an exquisite yet turbulent world in which we are routinely reminded that despite our best efforts at denying it, we are not invincible.

Yet even when we find ourselves cartwheeling, end over end, often struggling to determine which way is up, there is a love that refuses to leave us at the bottom of the sea. When Jesus told his friends that trouble would come, his statement wasn't finished. Rather, his next words were about having courage, taking heart, for "I have overcome the world" (John 16:23). The tumbling will not take us out; it will not do us in. It will not last forever. And when the tumbling finally subsides and we find ourselves coughed out onto the shore, if we are wise, we will notice we've been changed. We have not only survived the tumbling; we have been refined into a smoother, gentler version of ourselves. The tumbling of suffering and pain will, if we let it do its work, result in something beautiful.

I also wish the smoothing of my soul could happen without the pain that accompanies the tumbling. How I wish God would reach down and rescue me from the surge, that I could simply carry on beneath a tranquil sea. Instead, God allows the tumble—for some of us much more than for others—which will be a mystery for as long as we walk this earth. The mystery of it runs throughout the natural world: new life comes as a replacement for something that has died. Jesus tried to explain this principle to his disciples with an agricultural illustration that they all would recognize: a wheat seed falls to the ground and dies so that more wheat will grow and produce more seeds.

I met with a young woman for her bimonthly spiritual direction session. After some initial lighthearted chatting followed by a moment of silence and prayer to prepare for our time together, I asked her to tell me how she was feeling about her spiritual life. After a moment or two of consideration, she provided a vivid word picture: "I just feel like there is so much background noise." I nodded in agreement: I know the feeling.

When my friend made her observation about "background noise," I encouraged her to talk about where all that background noise was coming from and to consider if there was something to pay attention to in the midst of it. She went on to discuss a friendship that was requiring more of her time and emotional energy than she had expected. Her desire to help her friend was genuine, but the ongoing nature of that friend's personal crisis was starting to take its toll, leaving the young woman feeling . . . tumbled.

While Jesus was certainly right about the persistent presence of trouble in the world, he knew about the deep, inner soul trouble that afflicts us all now and then. My friend did her best to describe the tumbling that was going on in her inner life—the trouble that was keeping her from clarity, a sense of well-being, and a lively connection with God. As her spiritual director, I believe my role is to enter into the tumbling with her in an effort to help her listen to her life and pay attention to how the tumbling is shaping her. Ultimately, it may even be to invite her into a deeper life with God. At the end of our time together, she had acquired some clarity in the form of a new determination to seek God in silence. The volume level of the background noise needed to be turned way down.

Too often, we move through the tumbling in our lives by denying its presence. We continue at a pace so rapid that we are robbed of the chance to learn and grow from challenging situations. Growth comes down to having the courage to let our lives teach us in all their tumultuous glory, an opportunity many people willingly embrace each time they come for spiritual direction. With that kind of courage in place, we begin to notice some of our rough edges wearing off. Ever so slowly, a smoother surface takes their place. We may find we are freer to love and be present—not only to God but to the many other souls that cross our paths. We might be surprised by the gentler, more patient version of ourselves that emerges now and then. Like the satisfaction my green stones gave my granddaughter as she held them to her face, we might become the cool, reassuring source of comfort to a friend who is going through a time of tumbling.

> Growth comes down to having the courage to let our lives teach us in all their tumultuous glory.

I have recognized bits of polishing in my own life, thanks to the spiritual direction that Iona has given me. I have grown in my understanding of how to seek and find God, and I have become more self-aware, alert to the current state of my mind and heart. Again, that is what a good spiritual director helps us do. It can certainly feel like tumbling; spiritual direction is a deeply personal and sometimes even chaotic experience. However, it helps us recognize the redemptive work of God in our lives, and it allows us to see the truth about who we are and what we have to offer the world.

But Iona is not the first spiritual director I've had. That was Margaret, years ago. I was working at a small magazine in the town where Cary was a seminary student. I heard Margaret speak at an event sponsored by the seminary, and I knew right away that she was a person I wanted in my life. She was an academic, a professor of music at the college across the street; she was married, without children ("but I have many spiritual children" she would answer whenever asked); and she was passionate about life with Jesus. When I listened to her speak, something in me snapped to attention, like a hungry child being called to dinner. We met every other week for two years as she walked me through a tumbling process that I'm certain was necessary for the polishing of my life.

Some of my other spiritual directors are writers whose books provide wise guidance in the absence of one who is present and accessible. One spring, I caught wind of a journaling class that Luci Shaw was teaching. I signed up immediately.

Shaw's poetry and instruction were thoroughly integrated with her Christian faith, and it was in that class that I received what is possibly the most significant piece of spiritual direction in my life: *pay attention*. This makes sense, of course, considering it was a journaling class. Shaw was helping us listen to our lives and to purposefully make note of what we heard and saw. She gave me the tools to be attentive to the tumbling and to not be afraid of it. "Write what you see," I remember her saying, "and what you don't see."

The natural world is worthy of our attention, for the obvious reason that we rely on the resources of our world to sustain life, but we are also spiritually richer when we pay attention to the world God has made and given to us to care for. The simple practice of taking notice of the life around us is inherently life-giving as well. When I notice the way the woods across the road from our house grow visibly greener with each passing day of early spring, it is an attentive act that inspires me. When I take extra time to applaud a young child's growing creativity or vocabulary, it is an attentive act that humbles me. When my husband and I verbally declare the sighting of the first firefly of the summer, it is an attentive act that brings me joy.

Why are such simple practices worth considering? Because the more we pay attention to other people and to the Creation around us, the less likely we are to be overtaken by toxic self-absorption. At the same time, there is immense value in giving ourselves attention. If we hope to grow in our understanding of where God is in our lives and who we are in response, we have to be willing to ask ourselves some rather penetrating questions. Ignatius of Loyola was a Christian teacher of old who would ultimately be canonized—named a saint—by the Catholic Church. He is known for the spiritual practices he created, one of which is a helpful exercise in self-examination.

These questions, which I have adapted from the work of Ignatius, are ones I return to and encourage others to consider at the end of each day, with the goal of becoming more attentive to the ways we are moving toward or away from God.

1. Did I notice God's presence anywhere today? Were there any moments of meaning or

special comfort that I would do well to ponder before I go to sleep?

2. **Were there parts of my day I can be especially grateful for?** Were there any ordinary or extraordinary examples of God's provision for me? Who were the people who enriched my life? Were there any moments of beauty, surprise, or delight?

3. **What role did my feelings play in this day?** What did my emotions reveal about what's important to me right now? Was there anything especially troubling that I might present to God for help? What was my general attitude toward myself, others, and God today?

4. **What was the most important part of my day, and why was it significant?** Did I receive any new insights as a result of that experience?

5. **What challenges or joys do I anticipate happening tomorrow?** Where might I ask for God's particular help in the day ahead? Are there any burdens or worries about the future that I am needlessly carrying?

When we allow ourselves to be guided and confronted by questions like these and are brave enough to respond with honesty, new avenues of growth can emerge.

Intentional self-examination can help us make better sense of the tumbling—the upending circumstances of our lives that seem to come to us senselessly. If we take time to reflect, as Ignatius suggests, we will learn to see the ways God is working in our lives, in spite of the tumbling. And a gentle, growing gratefulness will sprout in place of the weeds of bitterness and resentment.

Another way God has used spiritual direction in my life is through spiritual friendship. This is a beautiful Celtic concept, as the *anamchara*, or "soul friend," was a critical part of life in early Celtic monasteries like Columba's on Iona. Each monk in the monastery was expected to have a soul friend, and these pairs of monks often shared a cell. As abbot, Columba himself served as a soul friend—a confessor, an encourager, a listener, a pray-er.

I think this kind of spiritual director is perhaps the most treasured, for spiritual friends can walk through life together in an informal yet powerful way. Some spiritual friends utilize their relationship as a way to encourage each other in prayer, self-examination, and reflection. Others simply recognize that their relationship offers a unique opportunity for productive tumbling that results in polishing. At their most basic, spiritual friends are what their title implies: friends who nurture and guide each other in the ways of the Spirit.

Author Ian Bradley likens the Celtic concept of soul friendship to the way sponsors pair with participants in Alcoholics Anonymous or other organizations that seek to help and to heal. It is not directive but supportive, as any true friend should be. Contemporary life comes loaded with challenges, whether physical, mental, emotional, spiritual, or all of the above. No one should have to face the deepest questions of life on their own.

For many years, Sally has been a soul friend, an *anamchara*, to me, though for too long now our physical distance has made our connections less frequent. Not many of us know more than one or two such insightful souls, even in the course of a lifetime. But when we do connect, we pick up where we left off and rarely spend much time in pleasantries or trivialities—we get right to the heart and soul of things. I can confidently say Sally knows the deepest intentions of my heart. She practices the skill of paying attention and is therefore a consummate encourager and a devoted intercessor; I suspect she's offered more prayers on my behalf, and on behalf of my children, than anyone in my life. As George Eliot wrote, there is an "inexpressible comfort of feeling safe with a person; having neither to weight thoughts nor measure words, but to pour them all out, just as they are, chaff and grain together, knowing that a faithful hand will take and sift them, keep what is worth keeping, and then, with the breath of kindness, blow the rest away." That's the very definition of a soul friend, someone who makes our seasons of chaotic tumbling less jarring and who is the first to celebrate when the rough edges of our character show signs of becoming smoother. Soul friends are there to stand watch and pray, ready to help us through the next big tumble.

That's the very definition of a soul friend, someone who makes our seasons of chaotic tumbling less jarring and who is the first to celebrate when the rough edges of our character show signs of becoming smoother.

At a recent retreat on Iona, our group gathered one evening to discuss the key elements of the early Celtic expression of Christian faith, particularly on Iona, and why it is so historically rich and significant to us today.

As we closed our time and moved into more light-hearted chitchat, the topic of the Enneagram came up. Suddenly, everyone was talking at once, eager to engage in this topic. I mentioned how I was surprised to hear that the Enneagram was such a source of enthusiasm in the UK, since I had wondered if it was only a trend in the United States. Authors Ian Morgan Cron and Suzanne Stabile, who write about the Enneagram, say this tool can help us ensure that our interactions with other people are healthy rather than harmful. The Enneagram teaches us how to recognize the way our personality or temperament is uniquely created and how those very beautiful characteristics can also get us into trouble. According to the Enneagram, there are nine basic personality types (*ennea* is Greek for "nine"), and each type interfaces with the world in its own way. The emergence of the Enneagram has been met with wild enthusiasm in some quarters and skepticism or glib dismissal in others.

It was intriguing to hear my British friends talk about how helpful the Enneagram had been to them and how their churches had engaged in exploring it with regard to faith and spirituality. One gentleman claimed that gaining a new understanding of the Enneagram had literally changed his life, giving him tools he needed to navigate some particularly rough relational waters. I guess you could say the Enneagram proved to be helpful in a time of tumbling.

In my work in spiritual direction, I have many questions about the Enneagram, and I am eager to learn more. It shows me the importance of seeing ourselves as we really are—the rough edges and the smooth—and to likewise see others with the same compassion that God has for them. It isn't necessarily an enjoyable experience. When I tune in to a podcast about the Enneagram, I love how often the hosts engage their audience by saying, "Okay, we have to give you the bad news about yourself before we can give you the good news." If we want to see real growth happen, we have to face the truth about ourselves: some tumbling is involved first. So if you're under the impression that the Enneagram is just another device to help people feel good about themselves, you'd best buckle up. No one can charge the Enneagram with sugarcoating.

I think we crave tools like the Enneagram because we long to understand what is going on in the deepest parts of our souls. Learning about my "type" has given me a way to see the rough edges that need burnishing. One aspect of type five—which I'm pretty sure fits me—is that when we are under stress, we tend to have anxiety about diminishing resources, whether they be internal or external. Fives have only so much energy to spare, so they tend to allocate it carefully. This fear of diminishing resources is not a self-fulfilling prophecy proclaimed by the Enneagram; it is absolutely, undeniably true for me and has been all of my life. I am afflicted with a general fear that I will not have enough, whether energy, wisdom, money, or time. For example, I worry about having the ability or the grace to take care of aging parents, as well as my own husband, who is vulnerable to the capricious manifestations of the multiple sclerosis he carries in his body. And—true confession—I am overwhelmed at the prospect of having a group of people to my house for dinner. For many people, maybe most people, this is a no-brainer. But for whatever reason, I find the prospect of creating a meal for others completely intimidating; I fear I don't have the energy, creativity, or money to do it well. I can stand up and speak in front of a thousand people with no problem, even with little warning. But the idea of hosting people for a meal that I am responsible for preparing is enough to provoke a migraine. Ask my husband—I'm only moderately exaggerating.

This past year has been a tumbling one, particularly in my work. I've been put in positions of leadership that at times have caused me to wonder if God will provide what I need, if I will have enough. It can be a rather unsettling process that has revealed a helpful truth: I *don't* have enough. I am a limited human, with only so much to give. I cannot be all things to all people and am not being asked to be. Freedom! Like my friend at the Argyll retreat who claimed real growth and healing, I admit that the Enneagram has forced me to look at myself differently, to have more grace and patience with myself, and to consider the origins of the expectations I have. That change of mindset is evidence that I am responding to the tumbling, that I'm growing smoother, being polished by the Spirit of God.

My bowl of green stones from St. Columba's Bay reminds me that God's process of forming me may feel perilous at times and that it is a lifelong ordeal. They also urge me to believe that something glowing and beautiful will likewise be the result, that perhaps my life can serve as a smooth stone in someone else's hand . . . a source of calm, cool stillness in the midst of their own turbulent sea.

QUESTIONS FOR SPIRITUAL DIRECTION

1. Think about the state of your soul five or ten years ago and compare it to today. Do you feel more inclined toward God or less?
2. Are there any examples of the polishing process in your life? What were the results?
3. Which people (like a spiritual director) or tools (like a special book or the Enneagram) have helped you process the tumbling in your life?

6

WHITE STONE

A New Name

And now here is my secret, a very simple secret:
It is only with the heart that one can see rightly;
what is essential is invisible to the eye.

—Antoine de Saint-Exupéry, *The Little Prince*

My second-grade teacher, Mrs. Crabtree, was perfection personified. She was young and kind, with a broad smile and big brown eyes like buttons. I adored her.

One day, when the whole class was silently working at our desks, she suddenly called my name and asked me to step out in the hall with her. I felt more than a little nervous, wondering what this could be about. The last thing I wanted in the world was to disappoint Mrs. Crabtree.

She leaned over and looked at me with her chocolate eyes and quietly asked, "Tracy, did you give Cathy your crayons?" Cathy was a girl in my class. Earlier, I had told my mom that it seemed like Cathy's family didn't have much money (funnily enough, we didn't either) and that I had noticed Cathy didn't have her own crayons. My mom suggested I give her mine and promised that we'd find some others for me.

I sheepishly admitted to Mrs. Crabtree that yes, I had given my crayons to Cathy. I shuddered, certain that I had crossed some unseen boundary line of deviancy. To my surprise, she said, her smile as warm as Christmas, "Tracy, that was a kind thing to do. I'm very proud of you." I felt the same kind of heat in my face that comes with extreme embarrassment, except this time it was from satisfaction: the teacher that I loved had noticed me.

***

The Gospel of John tells the story of someone who was seen in a life-altering way. Nathanael was a friend of one of Jesus's newest and most enthusiastic followers, Philip. In his eagerness, Philip told Nathanael about this new teacher. In fact, Philip boasted that this wasn't just any teacher—he made the audacious claim that Jesus was the very person they had all learned about growing up in Hebrew school. Jesus was the one that Moses and the other biblical prophets wrote about . . . and he was right there, walking among them.

Seeing Nathanael's skepticism (and who can blame him?), Philip urged him to come see for himself. When the moment came and Jesus encountered Nathanael, sure enough, Jesus spoke like a prophet, declaring this friend of a friend to be a man of integrity—which was a little strange, considering they had never met before.

Nathanael, astonished, asked, "How do you know me?" Jesus responded that he had *seen* Nathanael approaching and that he had *seen* him earlier while he was sitting under a tree. Jesus noticed Nathanael and talked about him like he was known. Overcome with emotion, Nathanael admitted that Philip was right: this must be the Son of God (John 1:43–51).

This story helps us understand what is involved in being seen and being known. Jesus sees Nathanael, a man who doesn't lie; Nathanael in turn sees Jesus and knows he is Divine.

We do not have the miraculous powers of seeing immediately past the surface as Jesus does. What we do have is the ability to pay attention. We give each other a gift when we see each other: when we take notice of the person sitting in the back row alone in church, when we notice small acts of kindness and call them out in an affirming way, or when we make eye contact and smile at the checkout person at Walmart.

To acknowledge one another is one of the most powerful ways of giving love.

When we purposely put our phones out of the way so we can see the person in front of us without our screens rudely obscuring the view, we have the chance to see and to know. But it's all too easy to forget to pay attention, as I realize when I remember all the times I have walked past students on our campus and thought to myself, "Oh, she was a student in my class last year . . . but what is her name?"

To acknowledge one another is one of the most powerful ways of giving love. If I am paying attention, I will notice what others around me are doing. Who in my life needs to be called out into the hall and told that their good work, their kindness, their unselfishness has been noticed?

My guess is that I overlook them far too often.

In our quest to better know ourselves, we can take comfort that God is already acquainted with every detail. Psalm 139 reminds us that not only are we seen, but we are known:

> You have searched me, Lord,
> and you *know* me.
> You *know* when I sit and when I rise;
> you *perceive* my thoughts from afar.
> You *discern* my going out and my lying down;
> you are *familiar* with all my ways.
> Before a word is on my tongue
> you, Lord, *know* it completely. (Psalm 139:1–4,
>   my emphasis)

There are so many descriptors here of the ways God knows and understands us and is surprised by nothing. Jesus immediately knew Nathanael was "a true Israelite in whom there is no deceit." The words "in whom" are important. Throughout the Gospels, we see how Jesus knew the deepest, innermost condition of people's souls. For example, he knew the deep interior of a Samaritan woman he met at a local well, including that her life story featured five husbands and a potential sixth; without shaming her, he offered her living water. And when he met a tax collector named Zacchaeus, he already knew the man's deception and thievery and ate dinner with him nonetheless. Jesus had a full grasp of what was in people, for better and for worse.

Who in your life knows what is *in you*? Who knows not only what you've done and where you've been but also your deepest secrets—and loves you still?

Here is a bit of what is *in me*, of which God is well aware.

I have always been a mix of extremes: on the one hand confident in many things, on the other anxious and fearful. For most of my life, I have kept my fears and worries inside, sharing them with no one. And although I have believed in Jesus for as long as I can remember and have heard him and his messengers saying "Do not fear" over and over in the Bible, worry and fear have battered my soul.

In my first year working in ministry to college students, my inner anxiety—what was *in me*—began to raise its ugly head in pronounced ways. I experienced small panic attacks, hyperventilation, and claustrophobia at inopportune moments. Just to drive the car through a car wash required a force of will.

As time passed, I grew increasingly worried about my ability to maintain my family and work responsibilities. I sought the help of a counselor and a medical doctor. I know this is a common story—I'm not telling you anything you haven't heard from someone else. But not many people know this about *me*.

However, Jesus does know, of that I am certain. *He sees me and he knows me.* I only need to remind myself of this truth every day. Maybe you do too.

I've created a small tradition for myself when I come to Iona.

Hiking down to Columba's Bay is a priority at some point in the week, hopefully on a day when the weather is cooperative. Even when wind and rain make an appearance, a flask of hot tea shared with a friend on the shore makes the extra bit of discomfort worth it.

The journey to Columba's Bay is about two miles from the Argyll Hotel down to the south end of the island. That is where it is believed that Columba and his friends first landed. In addition to the multicolored, sea-smoothed stones you've already read about, this beach contains many pure-white stones, which I like to gather. A gentleman who was part of one of my Iona pilgrimage groups said that if I keep bringing rocks home from Iona, there will be no Iona left. Cheeky.

The white stones serve a specific purpose, fulfilled once I'm back in the States and in my office at the university. I take out my black fine-point pen and in my best Celtic lettering inscribe them with "Iona," followed by the year of the visit. They congregate on my bookshelf where I can see, at a glance, the documentation of all of my Iona days.

The idea came to me as I read the book of Revelation, in which John of Patmos proclaims the vision he has received from God about who we are: "To the one who is victorious, I will give some of the hidden manna. I will also give that person a white stone with a new name written on it, known only to the one who receives it" (Revelation 2:17). Now, the Revelation is complex and mysterious, and I do not want to imply that I have any special insight into the original meaning of this particular passage. However, the image of Jesus giving a white stone with a new name on it is a compelling one. It provides a metaphorical way of reminding me that Jesus sees and knows me not only as I am now but as I will be.

With this in mind, when we are at Columba's Bay, I encourage my pilgrimage groups to look for a white stone among the multicolored stones that blanket the beach. When we return to the Argyll for reflection and prayer together, I challenge them to ask God, "Who am I?"

God knows what is in us in ways we often don't know ourselves. Our self-awareness is too often limited to the unhealthy comparisons that we make using social media. There are forces in the world that presume to know who we are, but this is often a far cry from what Jesus sees in us. If I really want to know the truth about myself, I sometimes have to do something radical, like take a day of silence or spend a weekend at my local Benedictine monastery—or go to an island on the other side of the world to be able to hear him tell me the answer . . . to receive from God a white stone with my new name.

And guess what? Every time I ask, God responds, and I write that name on a white stone so I won't forget the insights I've been given. "Dear One" was a response I received one time, just when I felt the need to be reminded of how God felt about me as his child. (I have always envied Lucy in the Chronicles of Narnia and her experience of hearing Aslan use that term of endearment for her.) "Beloved" was a new name I received another time on Iona. There does seem to be a pattern to God's names for me, the names I need to be reminded of.

Learning who I am isn't a one-time lesson; it's an ongoing spiritual practice to ask and receive. One October, I sat in the lounge at the Argyll Hotel, having just had breakfast with friends who were leaving that day. I let the words I was reading settle in as I sat by the window, watching the choppy waves of Iona Sound, erratic in the wind; the ferry carrying my friends was almost to the other side of the channel to Mull.

> Learning who I am isn't a one-time lesson; it's an ongoing spiritual practice to ask and receive.

I thought about how choppy my life had felt since I was last on Iona, just one year previous, and how befuddled I had been over the question of my place in the world. For most of my life, I have tried to follow where I think God is leading, relinquishing my own self-directed desires. After so many years of that kind of pursuit, you'd think I'd have greater confidence by now. You'd think I'd have an easier time of sensing when God says, "This is the way, walk in it."

No, I do not. The internal wrestling that ensues is exhausting. And it can take so, so long for the choppy waters to become smooth again.

On that morning in the Argyll Lounge, God compassionately reminded me again of a fundamental truth that I should know by now: that he sees me and knows me. "I will give you a new name," I read in Revelation. "I will give you a new name," I heard God say (Revelation 2:17).

So I opened my hand.

Where do we go to find out who we really are?

You don't have to travel to a remote island, that's for sure. The experience my group members have hiking down to St. Columba's Bay is spiritually meaningful as they look for a white stone to keep and as they spend time at that bay asking God to help them understand who they are. But it is the kind of spiritual practice that can be entered into anywhere—even if you are in the middle of the Great Plains, far from any stone-tumbling body of water.

Fortunately, there are rocks to be found just about everywhere, stones that God can use to speak to you on a quiet day about who you are. Take a long stroll in a nearby park or down a country road. Walk down a busy street with your eyes peeled for a small expression of God's love for you—if not a stone, then perhaps another small object, like a leaf, a seed-pod, or a feather. Pick that small thing up and hold it in the palm of your hand. And ask God to remind you what he sees in you.

Be still.

Wait.

Listen.

Perhaps you will want to write on your object, like my pilgrims write their new name on their white stone. Let it be a way to receive God's love for you. When we are open to that healing truth, we don't need anyone or anything else to tell us who we are.

Because we know.

QUESTIONS FOR SPIRITUAL DIRECTION

1. *What has the process of discovering your identity been like for you? What have you learned about yourself?*

2. *How has that affected the way you think about God?*

7

VIKING SHIP

Facing the Enemy

I would like to beg of you, dear friend . . . to have patience with everything that remains unresolved in your heart. Try to love the questions themselves, like locked rooms and like books written in a foreign language.

—Rainer Maria Rilke

A few years ago, I was on Iona as a participant on a retreat. I fully embraced the space to pay attention to whatever God might have for me there.

One afternoon with extra time, I recognized the impulse to *go*—that Celtic longing to set out on a journey on a path known only to God. In the spirit of the ancient Celtic *peregrini*, ancient monks like Columba who left their homes and families to go on a spiritual pilgrimage, I layered up, zipped up, laced up, and headed out, not knowing where the Spirit would take me.

I instinctively headed north, past the heart of the village and the abbey. I walked by a familiar stone cross to my right, silhouetted against the eastern shore. The sea bore the deep gray of steel under ragged, layered clouds. The wind pushed me along as I followed the narrow but well-traveled paths through pastures dotted with sheep and a shaggy highland cow or two. I finally reached a squeaky wooden gate in a fence built to keep the herds from going rogue, its post worn smooth from the touch of so many kindred hikers.

As I've mentioned before, my husband and I, as college professors, have taken students to study abroad many times. When we do, we teach them to see the *place* we are visiting as their text. We want the bulk of the learning to come not only from their traditional texts but from the environment itself. We want them to "read" the landscape, the people, and the culture as well as the great books that have been written about the place.

On Iona that day, I found myself at the White Strand of the Monks, where there is indeed much to "read," and I'm sorry to say it is a story that does not end well. Juxtaposed against brilliant white sand marked with great boulders of red-and-green Lewisian gneiss is an ancient scene of terror. In the ninth century, on the northeastern edge of Iona, monks stared out to sea and recognized the dreaded shape of a Viking boat coming toward them. They would have instantly known their fate, for word had gotten out that the Viking raiders were making their presence known in Britain, plundering monasteries for their treasures and relics. Iona was attacked three times in quick succession, in 795, 802, and 806; after a two-decade reprieve, it was invaded again in 826.

My heart caught in my throat as I considered the horrifying scene. Such beauty and terror fused together in one place is beyond my ability to comprehend.

> The fears I face in my life must be confronted if I am to know more fully who I am.

As I stood there at the White Strand, completely alone, I fixed my gaze on the sea, pondering the plight of the monks who lived and died so sacrificially, unnecessarily. I reflected on the challenges of my own life, each worrisome and real: a husband with a chronic disease, children moving into adulthood, finances that only seem to stretch just far enough, to name just a few;

these were the fears that populated the Viking boat I envisioned coming toward me.

The fears I face in my life must be confronted if I am to know more fully who I am. I cannot understand the depths of God's love for me if my fears are constantly vying for my attention. I have to decide daily whose voice I'm going to give my attention to: the voice of God, or the voice of fear.

As a child, there were quite a few fears in my Viking boat, so to speak. I would fret about the house catching on fire, about being kidnapped on the way home from school, about my parents dying in a car crash. I was a ball of anxiety.

One of the ways I learned to overcome some of those childhood fears was to lean into the things I could do well. Which meant I also had to experience the painful discovery of the things I wasn't good at: math, for one, which escapes my grasp to this day, and sports. The former was realized by poor grades and frustration, the latter by humiliation.

Each year, our elementary school hosted a "field day," abandoning academics to create a mini-Olympics out on the playground. I absolutely dreaded it. My mom loved to tell the story of me heading out the front door for school that day and turning to her with these words: "Don't expect any miracles."

Meanwhile, my best friend Laverne was an athletic phenom. Each year, Laverne ended field day covered with the blue ribbons she had won, each one pinned to her clothing and flapping proudly in the breeze. She was the fastest, the strongest, the most coordinated of anyone in the third grade. Laverne's dad played for the Houston Oilers. She clearly inherited some superlative DNA.

On the other end of the athletic spectrum was me. I walked in the door at the end of the day, evidence of my fulfilled prophecy affixed to my chest: each student in my class received a pathetic ribbon representing our final standing in the interclass tug-of-war competition (as if my scrawny arms had made a contribution). But I wasn't bitter about it. This was helpful information for me: I was not an athlete and never would be. And that was okay, because I learned there were other things I was good at.

I discovered I could draw—pretty well, in fact. Over the years, I won art contests and earned my teachers' confidence when something creative was needed in class. I also found that I could write. The same year of my epic field-day fail, my teacher chose my short story as the best in the class. (I was awarded two new pencils as a prize—not as glorious as blue ribbons, but it was something.) And a few years after that, I learned I could sing. From junior high through college, I auditioned for various vocal groups and solos and succeeded at every one of them.

It is helpful to know what you're naturally good at and to lean into those skills and develop them. The more you limit yourself to doing only what you're good at, the less likely it is that you will be a failure . . . at least in my way of thinking. For as long as I can remember, I have only applied, tried out, or signed up for things that I know I won't fail at. I wasn't motivated by the promise of success; I was galvanized by my fear of failure.

Practitioners in spiritual direction and formation know—as any good parent, coach, or trainer knows—that failure can be an effective teacher. We grow by learning from our mistakes. Our character is strengthened when we learn to push through rejection. The testing of our faith produces perseverance. I know all this, yet I avoid failure like the plague. Why is that?

It's not that I'm afraid I won't measure up to God's requirements for heaven. But I do fear I will fail at being a good steward while I'm here on this earth.

There is significant potential for failure in every area of my life (as there is in yours, I'm sorry to say). I'm afraid of failing my grandchildren and my great-grandchildren by leaving them an uninhabitable planet. I'm afraid of failing the people God loves by not speaking out more boldly on behalf of justice for the "least of these." I'm afraid I won't have what it takes to be faithful for the long haul. Shall I continue?

The thought of failing in these and so many other ways makes my head ache and my stomach churn—which is literally true; some months after my day on the White Strand, I found myself in the hospital with a bleeding ulcer. I know this sounds a bit dramatic, but nonetheless it is true.

That day on the White Strand had me quaking a bit as my Viking ship of doom figuratively rowed toward me, closer and closer. And that is when I heard the Spirit of God say, *Be braver.* It wasn't an audible voice, but it was an unmistakable one.

What the monks of Iona faced at the White Strand all those centuries ago is far more horrific than anything I am likely to experience. As of this writing, I've not experienced anything close to martyrdom. But in the minds of the ancient Celtic Christians of Ireland and Scotland, to truly love God was to be willing to sacrifice all, to relinquish one's grip on earthly success, and to embrace the way of the cross. The story of the White Strand of the Monks challenges us to face down the fears we have—not just fear of physical death like the monks but any fears that prevent us from flourishing.

What are those fears in your life? What keeps you up at night? I'm certain you do not literally have a ship of Vikings coming toward you, but I'll bet you have a boatload of other fears that come barreling toward you in most unwelcome moments. Naming each of the fears in your Viking ship, one by one, is the first step in being able to confront them. Write them down in your journal. Admit them to a friend. Who do you have in your life who would walk around in that Viking boat with you, naming those fears and throwing them overboard? What if Jesus was the one you invited to come along?

Fear is a real and present enemy, and I will take every bit of ammunition God has for me to fight against it.

Being at the White Strand makes me feel like I've had a good talking-to. I need to get over myself, to try new things, to be willing to fail, to be embarrassed even. *Be braver.* When a good idea comes and I'm tempted to shove it aside for fear of failure, I think, *Be braver.* When a chance arises to engage with people very unlike me and I'd much rather hide in the shadows, I think, *Be braver.* When the cause of justice has been blatantly ignored and I have the opportunity to speak up about it, I hear those words nudging me forward: *Be braver.*

A few months ago, I was once again on the White Strand of the Monks. It was a crystal-blue kind of day, the kind where Iona sparkles. With the exception of one family at the south end of the beach, I was alone. I could see the silhouettes of three or four children climbing on the rocks, their delighted squeals overpowering the sound of gently rolling waves.

> When the cause of justice has been blatantly ignored and I have the opportunity to speak up about it, I hear those words nudging me forward: *Be braver.*

I found a me-sized nook in the line of rock protruding from the sand and sat down to enjoy the sea and ponder the things God was saying to me during that visit to the island. Greylag geese flew overhead, honking. The air smelled of salt and seaweed and damp earth. It was a perfect day for peace and prayer and the listening I needed to do.

Suddenly, I noticed a massive gray cloud, heavy with rain, rapidly approaching from the south, the wind urging it along until it was right over me and my rocky nook. Gone was the bright light of the sun that had followed me to the beach. Now leaden drops of rain dove into the sand around me, each landing with a *pop-pop-pop*, pelting the hood of my waterproof jacket, soaking my jeans.

As they say in the UK, there was nothing for it. There was nowhere to go for shelter. I just had to wait it out and deal with the disappointment that there would be no leisurely listening for the Spirit of God on the historic beach that day. With the lower half of my body wet to the bone (the top half protected, in a manner of speaking, by my waterproof jacket), I stood up from my nook and quietly grumbled about how wet I'd gotten in such a short amount of time. The next thing I knew, a beam of sunlight pierced the clouds behind me, the light appearing as quickly as it had departed.

A spectacular rainbow stood in front of me, its brilliant glow plunging into the waves.

The rain continued in earnest. I knew I should give up, get back on the trail back to the hotel and get into some dry clothes, but the glory of the rainbow held me there, transfixed.

I finally succeeded in turning away from it and tromped through the field, my wet shoes squeaking against the long blades of grass with every step. Soaked and shivering, I happened upon a British couple standing in the field, every bit as soaked as I was, looking out over the sea toward the now fading rainbow. Just as I was about to comment about our lovely day being spoiled by the rain shower, the woman looked at me and, with a broad grin, exclaimed, "Wasn't that fabulous?"

She was right. There on a beach once soaked in the blood of the saints, we experienced a cleansing rain and the color of promise.

To me, the experience was a reminder that God will not let the enemy have the final word—no matter how vicious the invader or persistent the storm.

With that assurance, we can all afford to be braver.

QUESTIONS FOR SPIRITUAL DIRECTION

1. *What are the "Vikings" coming toward you? How might God be asking you to respond to those fears?*

2. *Who in your life has served as an example of courage in the face of fear? What have you learned from them?*

3. *How has God redeemed your experiences of failure?*

8

COLUMBA'S TEARS

Godly Grief

Sometimes, you don't realise the weight you are carrying until you come to a quiet, ancient place of unburdening.

—Dara McAnulty

When my Iona pilgrimage groups are charged with finding a white stone amid the untold thousands of colorful stones on Columba's Bay, I give myself a secret challenge. I go to remember the saint himself, who is an inspiration to me as a leader, an artist, a pastor, and a person longing to grow in prayer. I go to sit with my pilgrim friends, enjoying unhurried conversation as we walk along and a thermos of hot tea when we arrive. I go to drink in the refreshing sea breeze that wafts off the mighty waves as they crash onto the shore.

But my secret ambition is to find the stones the locals call Columba's tears.

These pear-shaped pieces of green serpentine are so highly polished by the sea that they appear luminous. When held up to the sun, they glow. They can be as small as a pinky fingernail and are often hiding underneath larger stones, thanks to the great force of the waves that push them deeper into the shore. Legend says that if you keep one in your pocket, it will protect you from drowning.

I tend to search for Columba's tears with determination, wanting to add to my collection. As I do, I wonder if their name, when combined with their rarity and obscurity, suggests something important about grieving. Why are these "tears" so hard to find? Why are my own?

I am not a crier; I never have been. Everyone else in my family is a certifiable weeper, including my husband. I am clearly the oddball, sitting dry-eyed on the couch while the rest of the family sits in puddles in front of *Les Misérables*.

What troubles me about my lack of emotional expression is that I can't seem to squeeze out a tear when things are truly painful, like when there is a death. I endured my mother's entire memorial service without crying. I have been with students as they learn of the death of a friend or loved one, absorbing their flood of tears but not adding my own. I can watch documentaries about 9/11 and emerge completely dry-eyed.

However, I do experience what I call "small tears" fairly frequently. When one of our university students from Central America speaks about how their college experience equipped them and challenged them in profound ways and how they will take their skills back to their home country where they will lead and serve, I am filled with amazement and experience small tears. Or when a student sits in my office and shares with me what it's like to live their life—to be gay or Black or autistic or profoundly lonely—I am humbled and honored and experience small tears. These individuals, with their victories, struggles, determination, personal growth . . . these inspire me and fill my heart with wonder at the ways God works in the human soul. These students evoke small tears because I am honored to share in their honesty, sorrow, and compassion in some way.

Whether my tears are large or small, I'm learning to see them as signals—signposts that invite me to step into someone else's sacred story. Such a step requires new levels of self-sacrifice. To willingly listen to a fellow human recount their stories of pain is not an experience we naturally long to have. To bear one another's burdens, as the Bible urges us to do, means that we are being asked to carry something heavy, something uncomfortable. Tears may indicate that such a sacrifice is being accepted; conversely, the lack of tears may reveal my unwillingness to enter into the pain my friend is experiencing.

It's important to pay attention to the difference as we move from inward examination (Who am I?) to outward action (What can I offer the world?). This is why Ignatius's tools for self-examination are so helpful. If we can identify the emotions we are feeling, we can better recognize what those emotions are teaching us and more sensitively enter into another's pain.

My youngest daughter, Langley, inherited the DNA of a long line of criers. Every time she and her husband, Jake, say goodbye after a visit with us, her poor tear ducts kick into gear. They love their life in Nashville, but the goodbyes rip her tender heart in two. Does she wonder how I can seem so cold and callous as I hold her tight, how I am so seemingly unaffected? I think about this every time we say goodbye.

By contrast, I am the stereotypical firstborn child, the one who feels the need to hold things together when the rest of the family, the church, the university, or the solar system is threatening to implode. My default response to weep-worthy events is to stubbornly refuse to use up any of the emotional energy that's available to everyone around me. I somehow believe that if I break down just a little, I will be making the problem worse than it already is. I subconsciously adopt the British stance: Keep Calm and Carry On. Stiff upper lip and all that.

There's a story in the Gospels about Jesus grieving. When he first heard that his friend Lazarus was seriously ill, he didn't appear too concerned. He authoritatively declared that Lazarus's illness would not end in death—a statement that seemed to legitimize his decision to wait for two days before traveling two miles to see Lazarus and his sisters, Mary and Martha.

Jesus loved these three siblings, and they deeply loved him. It was natural that Mary and Martha would call for Jesus when their brother was sick. But why didn't he immediately pop over to Bethany when it would have taken him only forty minutes to get there on foot from Jerusalem? Other people made the trip; Jews from Jerusalem had come to comfort the two sisters. Unfortunately, the women watched their brother die and be buried, all without the company of the One who was their friend, the One they believed could have healed her brother.

And then comes the shortest verse in the New Testament: "Jesus wept." Those two words convey an ocean of love, an expansive heart that carries the all-knowing wisdom of the Divine.

When Jesus finally did arrive, Mary fell at his feet, weeping: "Lord, if you had been here, my brother would not have died."

That would have given Jesus cause for reflection. When he sees Mary and her friends crying, "he was deeply moved in spirit and troubled" when he got this report (John 11:33).

"Where have you laid him?" Jesus asked.

"Come and see, Lord," they replied.

And then comes the shortest verse in the New Testament: "Jesus wept." Those two words convey an ocean of love, an expansive heart that carries the all-knowing wisdom of the Divine. And in that deep knowing, Jesus was aware of death and the human condition in ways we surely cannot imagine. God knows this is not the way it was meant to be. Brothers were not meant to die, friends were not meant to be disappointed, loss was not meant to be part of life.

If anyone should be expected to hold things together when life gets hard, to provide stability and assurance for others, and to exhibit a calming disposition for the benefit of people who are suffering, it's surely Jesus—yet Jesus was obviously moved and deeply troubled. *He wept.* He did not restrain his emotions. This makes me consider the role of weeping with others. Is there something I'm missing when I suppress my tears? Is it possible that public crying might be a way of showing love . . . that it could be a healing way of being with others?

Those mourning the death of Lazarus invited Jesus to "Come and see." This is the same invitation Jesus frequently offers throughout the biblical accounts of his life. It is a prompt to enter into a story in process, whether it be a story of grief, as in Mary's and Martha's case, or of celebration. When we are willing to come and see, we accept the human call to empathy. We've all been urged to walk in someone else's shoes, for only then can we hope to make a helpful difference in the world. How can I possibly know what a person needs if I don't make the effort to better understand the conditions in which they find themselves? How can I know how to encourage or support them if I don't have a grasp on the challenges they are facing? Our inclination to rush in and fix things may reveal our desire to help; it may also expose a low-grade carelessness that doesn't want to put in the hard work of understanding.

In my work as a campus minister, I get to hear many wise, articulate, insightful thinkers who speak in our chapel program. But unfortunately, I was out of town when Jemar Tisby came to visit. Tisby, the author of *The Color of Compromise: The Truth about the American Church's Complicity in Racism*, was invited to speak to our mostly white campus about an understanding of diversity that is firmly rooted in the ways and teachings of Jesus. When I returned, the buzz on campus was that his had been an especially powerful message. It propelled some of our students to action, challenged them to think more deeply about their role in issues of racism . . . and frustrated a few students enough to walk out.

From my perspective as a spiritual director and struggling human, it was good to see some students had been prodded to self-reflection and action. I never set out to frustrate our students, but holistic spiritual formation is often the result of hearing a challenging, prophetic, correcting word. Such moments can rouse us out of our comfy spiritual slumber. The result, hopefully, is a greater desire to work together for the common good.

Intrigued by what I heard from students, I closed the door of my office to listen to Tisby's message via our university's website. I took a lot of notes.

Tisby spent a good bit of time recalling atrocities committed against people of color. Each traumatic example of what he called the "systematic defacing of the image of God" prompted a spectrum of emotional responses in me, from deep sadness, to anger, to horror, to heartbreak. Too many of the atrocities have involved church-going folks and many who, in their silence, were complicit.

The accounts of the killing and oppression of Black people have been with us for centuries, and it is all too easy to confine them to the history books. Not long ago, I visited a garden space and museum in nearby Tulsa that memorialized what history records as the 1921 Tulsa Race Riot, a massacre of an estimated three hundred people in the predominantly Black neighborhood of Greenwood. How can a person live in this region for twenty years and not know this horrific story?

More recently, I had the opportunity to be part of a live audience gathered to hear Bryan Stevenson, a social justice activist, author, and founder of the Equal Justice Initiative. In his book *Just Mercy*, he writes as a Christian lawyer urging his readers to consider the desperate need to reform our country's criminal justice system.

That night, hundreds of people gathered in the auditorium at Crystal Bridges Museum of American Art to hear Stevenson tell heart-wrenching stories of how men and women of color are legally misrepresented—victims of racial injustice that results in unfair or excessive incarceration.

And that is one among many issues that generates sympathy and passion—and a call for response. As I write this, our country is embroiled in divisions over serious problems at our southern border and the inhumane ways people seeking asylum are being treated there. Families are being separated, children are held in cages in unsanitary conditions, and medical treatment is unavailable or, worse, withheld intentionally. It is an overwhelming issue—and guidance from the Bible is clear. Matthew Soerens from

World Relief offers faith leaders compelling evidence for why Christians cannot turn a blind eye, pointing out that the Hebrew word that most closely aligns with *immigrant* shows up ninety-two times in the Old Testament, often alongside vulnerable groups like widows and orphans. God, he says, expressly loves those vulnerable people and commands his people to love them as well.

When I hear and am forced to confront these stories of the "defacing of the image of God," tears emerge: tears for the suffering of brothers and sisters, tears for our ongoing inability to make any lasting change, tears for my own ignorance—the ways I am all too easily able to go about my daily life, never having to worry if the color of my skin or my children's skin will make it dangerous to drive a car alone or walk through the streets of my small Southern town. I don't experience anxiety about being perceived as suspicious or dangerous because of my skin color. I have confidence that if I encounter legal issues, I will have fair representation.

What am I to do? What are we to do? These are the questions that all spiritual direction asks. These are the questions that should be asked in any guidance from a spiritual director, any sermon, commencement speech, or TED talk. When we meet our own tears, we are called to particularly ask what caused those tears. If we believe in a God whose image is present in every human being, regardless of their country of origin or the color of their skin, how do we create a more just world?

In the spirit of a good prophet, Jemar Tisby offered some strong direction. He started talking about Godly grief. Lament. Repent. *We need to cry.* This challenge is not about how many tears we cry but the quality of those tears—to not just cry once out of sympathy but cry out of *empathy.* Journalist Mark Honigsbaum agrees, challenging us to "make the imaginative effort to step into the shoes of another person and see things from their perspective." When we do that, "we become less capable of ignoring their suffering."

Only by imaginatively and purposefully placing ourselves in the shoes of the "other" can we hope to combat the pain that is unjustly, and often systematically, inflicted on our brothers and sisters. People who have privilege must be willing to understand the depth of the pain of the Black community so that society will be motivated to make a change.

If we hope that people bearing the image of God are not shot because of the color of their skin . . .

If we hope that people bearing the image of God are not unjustly incarcerated because of the color of their skin . . .

If we hope that people bearing the image of God are not afraid to drive their car or go to certain stores or send their kids to school because of the color of their skin . . .

Then we need to get over ourselves and cry. We need to weep with those who weep, as the Bible puts it. For me, personally—the dry-eyed stalwart in the room—I need to offer my Columba's tear, even though it is small, to express my desire to understand what that kind of pain is like. To offer a tear is the first step in declaring that I cannot, I will not, let this happen to my brothers and sisters anymore.

Saying in our own imperfect way, "I am here and I see your pain . . . and I'm so desperately sorry," is an important first step toward healing and reconciliation. But we have to take that step. And there are other steps to follow. Words of empathy fail when we do not stand alongside our brothers and sisters, when we do not speak out.

To add my tears to the grief in the room is to fully participate in collective sorrow.

I work with a brilliant scholar who bears the burden of racial injustice very personally. When I express my frustration in not knowing how best to engage in racial reconciliation as a white person, she graciously reminds me that the white community does not have to do this perfectly. Even the smallest expressions of empathy can become glowing orbs of light, a treasure in a grieving hand, a way to say in our own imperfect way, "I am here and I see your pain . . . and I'm so desperately sorry." It is an important first step toward healing and reconciliation.

But we have to take that step. And there are other steps to follow. Words of empathy fail when we do not stand alongside our brothers and sisters, when we do not speak out.

My colleague's words give me courage to not be afraid of tears if they come, to not be afraid to step into the fray more.

We often speak of being "moved to tears" to begin healing work. This common phrase is more accurate than we know, because the tears themselves are not the end goal; the actions following the tears are what we need to hope for. It is true that to cry with one another is, in itself, a healing thing. Better still is when those tears set our hands and feet into motion. As a self-proclaimed noncrier, it is a fact that I have cried more—substantially more—over the last few months than I have over the last few years. The pain of the world grows closer and closer, as we have access to details around the clock. I can't help but cry, and they are no longer small tears.

In his *The Color of Compromise*, Jemar Tisby declares that if we hope to know reconciliation in our fractured world, we have to start with receiving truth: the truth about what has happened, what is happening, and our part in it. That truth is very painful to hear, and when I hear it, the big tears come. Truth, Tisby says, is the first step in a healing process that leads toward confession, then to repentance, and finally to reconciliation.

Recently, our campus held a memorial service. We gathered at 4 p.m. in the center of our campus on the stretch of grass and trees we call "the quad" and were led by students and faculty in a liturgy of lament in memory of a great atrocity— a massacre—that happened 101 years ago in our state. On September 30, 1919, white mob violence resulted in the deaths of five white people and at least two hundred Black men, women, and children—

another story that has somehow escaped my notice, even though I've lived in Arkansas now for more than twenty years.

The students and faculty who had visited Elaine, Arkansas, last year on an academic trip returned to our campus with the conviction that these were people who needed to be remembered. This was a story that needed to be told.

Thanks to their initiative, we listened to the story on the quad that day, grieving for the horrific loss, praying together, and remembering. We planted a tree in the quad, a tree of remembrance, with a plaque at its base: "We remember and deeply lament the deaths of these individuals made in the image of God and the racism and hatred that led to this event. While we may not be directly culpable for this event, we are responsible to remember and lament it, to repair the legacy of racism, and to work toward racial reconciliation and justice in our own time as a part of our calling to follow Jesus Christ."

Perhaps taking up the collective charge to keep telling the story, to keep remembering, is part of what being "moved to tears" means. May we have the humility required to enter into the process without fear.

Meanwhile, I will keep collecting my tiny green stones on Iona's southern shore. I will let Columba's tears remind me that crying is not only an appropriate emotional expression; lament is a biblical imperative. Weeping is a way of coming alongside the one who weeps, who has been abused, who has suffered loss. Our tears, small and imperfect as they are, can be powerful instruments of compassion, moving us to honor and stand by the image of God in every person.

QUESTIONS FOR SPIRITUAL DIRECTION

1. *What makes you cry, and why?*
2. *Is there someone you feel God might be asking you to empathize with? Who is it and what has caused their pain?*
3. *Where have you recently seen the image of God on the face of another human?*

III
WHAT CAN I OFFER
THE WORLD?

9

COORIE IN

Welcome

I believe that when all is said and done, all you can do is to show up for someone in crisis, which seems so inadequate.

—Anne Lamott

Never before had I traveled to Iona in such torrential rain.

It was autumn, so there was only a small handful of passengers aboard that day. Upon hearing the great "clunk" as the ferry met the jetty's edge, we prepared to disembark. As I left the boat, I pulled the two hoods of my layered jackets over my head and eyes and walked headfirst into the pelting rain. *So this is what the village is like in the off-season*, I thought: dreary, gray, and nearly deserted. I was one of only a few visitors that October day, and the weather seemed intent on demonstrating just why that might be true.

I slogged up the jetty, my jeans and feet soaked, head aching, hungry and not a little crabby after a long day of travel: train, ferry, bus, and the final ferry from Mull to Iona. Fortunately, the Argyll Hotel is but a stone's throw from the jetty, and my feet know the path well. I arrived at the front door of the hundred-year-old hotel and heaved my dripping suitcase and backpack into the hotel vestibule. Oh for a cup of tea and some dry socks.

I walked through to the front desk, passing an array of Wellington boots lining the floor of the entryway, all manner of rain gear hanging on pegs on the wall, and was startled by the sounds of boisterous laughter, clinking glasses, and delicious aromas. A wild banshee of a storm raged outside, but here inside the hotel dining room, there was warmth and light and frivolity. Think of the Green Dragon Inn in the Lord of the Rings, only with a tad more class, and you'll picture the scene perfectly.

"Coorie in," the Scots say. *Come in from the storm, be warm and dry. . . . Come and be cozy and well.*

I soon learned it was a wedding party; the ceremony had just taken place at the abbey. I found myself smiling as family and friends gaily shared stories and memories around their tables, the crackling fireplace emanating the comforting scent of burning peat.

God invites me to *coorie in* to this way of being present, to receive the comforting blanket of a holy presence even in the midst of raging storms. It's not permission to deny that such troubles exist or to turn a blind eye to the needs of others. Rather, it is an offer of hospitality, of simple comforts, followed by God's bidding to replicate that invitation for others. How might I better be a place of comfort and welcome to others? What can I do to assure others that they can come in from the storm and *coorie in*? There is hope in our togetherness as fellow image bearers of God, especially when we invite Christ to stand at the center of that togetherness.

In the midst of the book of Revelation, we are given a vision of a great future day when "a great multitude that no one could count" will stand before God's throne. They'll come "from every nation, tribe, people and language" and praise God together with the angels (Revelation 7:9). It's the New Jerusalem, the heavenly city.

Iona's hospitality has given me a picture of this New Jerusalem, in which God will make all things new. In the very ordinary experiences of laughter around a fire or a hot cup of tea, there is holiness; these tastes and smells and textures breathe life into even the dreariest of days. In them I begin to catch a glimpse of a New Heaven and a New Earth. I can start to imagine what it will be like when, one day, everyone belongs and has an honored place.

While we await that day, we can invite others to *coorie in*. We can choose to embody the safety and security that a monk's cell illustrates and swing the door open wide with welcome. I have friends that are particularly gifted in this way. Tim is always generous with his invitations to come and share dinner with him and his wife, Pam—dinner often being one of his homemade pizzas adorned with exotic cheeses and herbs. Or Becci, who is probably the most fantastic cook I know but also makes everything artistically beautiful. One of my favorite days of the year is when Becci invites a group of her friends and colleagues to an exquisite Christmas lunch served in her home. The food is beyond delicious, and the conversation is nourishing. Becci knows how to invite us to *coorie in*.

A former student I know has befriended a foreign family that has relocated to northwest Arkansas. She is a white American Christian; the family are Afghani Muslims. She has visited them every Friday for the last eight months, nurturing an authentic friendship with people too often dismissed as "other." I am awed at her willingness to step into spaces she is not naturally equipped for. She tells me that eating with them in their home, in their customary way (in the living room, not the dining room or kitchen, and using hands rather than flatware), has been a significant way of connecting with them. Driving them to the mosque every week, learning about their culture, and humbly listening to their stories has enriched her own life.

It's a curious thing, this reversed hospitality. By joining this foreign family in their home, my friend willingly enters into a space and a cultural expression that can potentially be quite uncomfortable for her. She does this so her friends will be most comfortable, where they can be at ease and share their culture with her. Sometimes the most hospitable thing we can do is allow someone else to show hospitality to us, even if it comes with discomfort for ourselves.

I most often feel that I fall quite short when it comes to the traditional understanding of hospitality, but my days and weeks on Iona have confirmed to me that we all have ways of inviting others to *coorie in*. God has uniquely gifted me to welcome others as well, and even though my efforts may not taste incredible or look pretty or seem brave, this is what I have to offer:

I can listen. The ability to really listen to someone else, and be listened to in turn, is a gift in itself. When is the last time someone really listened to you or let you verbally process your thoughts without fear of judgment? Who has freely given you the gift of time and attention, affirming that your story is in process and that it is sacred?

I can ask meaningful questions. Questions that address the deeper concerns in a person's life are a gift that demonstrates authentic interest and love. Meaningful questions can help a person grow in understanding who they are before God.

I can help others pay attention. We can be together in silence, waiting for the Holy Spirit to lead. We can try not to be in a hurry in order to pay attention to what God might be doing. This seems very simple, but that's precisely why it is a beautiful gift. When our time together is stripped of superfluous chatter and the generally rapid pace that most of us assume, there is finally space for God to get a word in edgewise.

Meanwhile, I can put the kettle on for tea and find something resembling a cookie to munch on. Despite my lack of Pinterest-worthy abilities, I want to create a safe place where you are welcome to talk about anything you like, whether trivial or intensely personal. I'm all ears, and I am genuinely interested in who you are and what you bring to this world.

Columba offered this kind of hospitality to his monks as well as to visitors to Iona who would come for spiritual nourishment and guidance. As we've seen, the founding abbot of Iona had a cell that was visually prominent so that all would know how to find him. From his cell, the abbot offered pastoral guidance, prayer, and comfort to his beloved monks. He also likely engaged in his own spiritual practices there, including chanting the Psalms and painstakingly copying the scriptures for use in worship.

Each of these aspects of Columba's life and ministry—pastoral care, prayer, and creativity—served to make his hut a place to *coorie*, a refuge for others and for himself that made the presence of God accessible in a deeply meaningful way.

As I search for a modern example, I think of the inimitable Fred Rogers. His genuine attention to "the least of these"—to children—has been noted by many. Mister Rogers made a strategic decision on his television program to switch his street shoes to sneakers and his sport jacket to a zip-up cardigan. With his gentle voice, his pleasant demeanor, and his very clear intention to never be in a hurry, his clothing signaled an invitation for his audience to *coorie in*.

In the same way that sneakers are more comfortable than business shoes and a cardigan is more comfortable than a sports jacket, we can discover gestures that communicate to others that they can relax in our presence, be themselves, and know that they are welcome and loved.

My spiritual director, Margaret, went out of her way to recognize what made each person unique, much like Fred Rogers did. I have a friend who is a good bit taller than most women. When Margaret met her, she said with her trademark enthusiasm, "Isn't it *wonderful* to be tall?" Margaret was herself taller than the average woman. She could have simply chosen to commiserate on all the ways that being taller than average might be a burden. Instead,

Margaret was a genuinely enthusiastic host, inviting my friend into her world where there was nothing better than being tall. She welcomed my friend into a figurative cell where anyone would want to live, especially tall people—because it's not just acceptable to be tall; it's *wonderful*.

This is a profound reminder to me of the many ways that hospitality is offered. In whatever manner we might use our gifts, the goal is the same: proximity, to lessen the distance between ourselves and others, no matter what they believe or don't believe. This can be physical distance, cultural distance, emotional distance, political distance, even spiritual distance. Decreasing that space does not deny our differences; it simply doesn't allow those differences to get in the way of loving others as we are called to do. Former first lady Michelle Obama did this in her Netflix documentary *Becoming*. The film featured highlights of her book tour, including clips of meet and greets with fans asking her to autograph her book. Obama's voice-over commentary described what viewers were seeing: her

> In whatever manner we might use our gifts, the goal is the same: proximity, to lessen the distance between ourselves and others.

determined effort to look each person in the eye as they arrived at her table. This was not only intended as a gesture of kindness but for the purpose of hearing their story, for conveying that, in that moment, they were the most important person in the room.

When Jesus was asked what the greatest commandment was, he said simply, "'Love the Lord your God with all your heart and with all your soul and with all your mind.' This is the first and greatest commandment. And the second is like it: 'Love your neighbor as yourself.' All the Law and the Prophets hang on these two commandments" (Matthew 22:37–40). Love God and love your neighbor. Invite people who are weary of walking through a broken world to *coorie in* to a kindness and welcome that will be irresistible.

"Come . . . and I will give you rest," says Jesus (Matthew 11:28).

"[Do] not giv[e] up meeting together," says the writer of Hebrews (10:25).

"Coorie in," I want to say to others, for Iona has said that to me.

Just as a good spiritual director should.

QUESTIONS FOR SPIRITUAL DIRECTION

1. Can you remember a time when you have known, beyond a shadow of a doubt, that you were welcomed and loved? What do you remember about it?
2. How do you express hospitality to others? What are your gifts for helping other people coorie in?

WHEESHT

The Silencing

Say but little and say it well.

—Gaelic proverb

The Argyll Hotel's front desk is also the reception area for its restaurant. While checking in for your much-anticipated stay, you'll likely see a member of the waitstaff carrying some artistic creation out of the kitchen for a lucky person in the dining room. On the shelf above the desk is an array of bottles exhibiting the various Scottish beverages available, including a bottle of ale labeled *WHEESHT*. The sight of this makes me giggle.

Getting the hang of the local vernacular in a place like Scotland can be a challenge, especially when accompanied by the distinctive Scottish accent.

Nothing betrays a visitor like having to ask for a phrase to be repeated three times.

For me and my family, that's been part of what feeds our affection for anything English, Scottish, or Irish. The bottle above the desk at the Argyll made me laugh because my sister, Wendy, and I love to work on our (badly done) Scottish accents, and a phrase we throw around frequently is *Haud yer wheesht!* This is a brilliant phrase whose sound perfectly matches its meaning—which is, essentially, shut up. The word *wheesht* comes from the Gaelic for "be quiet."

The word *wheesht* always pulls a smile out of me. But it is also a succinct expression of one of the most formative lessons Iona has taught me over time: if I desire a transformative connection with the God of the universe, I simply have to be quiet.

I've written elsewhere about the importance of silence in the life of faith, of purposefully entering into spaces and places where we can actually listen to God. That silence is essential for me, as I long to discern the voice of God—for direction, for assurance, for reminding me of who I am as his child. Our noisy culture makes this a challenge. And while much of that noise is life-giving and enriching (e.g., music, conversation, celebration), it is remarkable how rare the experience of true silence is. It's a challenge worth taking on, even if it means driving without music playing now and then, resisting the default compulsion to turn on the television, or going on our daily run without the earbuds. Embracing opportunities for silence and stillness—even if it's just five minutes a day— gives the Holy Spirit a chance to speak into a life that is often far too frantic and preoccupied.

Iona provides that space for silence and stillness in abundance. But as a good spiritual director, it has nudged me into a new consideration: not only do I need to *enter into* silence, but Iona is teaching me that I can actually *create* silence. There is an actual ministry offered to us in making spaces of silence for others. I don't mean directing silent retreats (which I love to do) or creating a prayer garden (I have a large backyard that cries out for it). No, Iona gives me a time-honored spiritual practice that both requires and nurtures humility in me.

While that cheeky ale bottle is a reminder of this lesson, Iona uses something much more substantial and lasting to make its stamp on my soul: the unofficial trademark of the island, Iona Abbey.

The abbey church has been restored thanks to many committed souls in the early twentieth century. The bulk of the work was completed under the direction of Rev. George MacLeod, founder of the modern-day Iona Community that hosts regular worship services at the abbey. All are welcome, including any residents, visitors, or tourists who might find themselves on the island. In the summer months, services are held in the abbey church each morning and evening; in the off-season, the drop in the temperature and the number of visitors force the group into smaller quarters—the Michael Chapel, which stands just behind the abbey.

I go to services in the abbey as often as I can when I am on the island and am especially keen to take my summer pilgrimage groups to experience the creative, thoughtfully designed services they hold there each evening. I am routinely struck by the community's mindfulness that people from all over the world may be in attendance. Sitting in the choir stalls, I am not surprised to hear voices around me from Germany, France, or Africa, and of course I hear all manner of British dialects. There is also a wide swath of religious traditions, likely including people who have no faith tradition at all. This does not result in a mushy, everything-goes spirituality. On the contrary, the Iona Community remains committed to credal Christianity as it would have been expressed in Columba's day.

I've considered this deeply over the years, this impressive ability to bring diverse people together in such a meaningful way. And I've realized that every word holds great weight in the worship services. Each word that is spoken, sung, or prayed has been carefully planned; not one is superfluous. Any directions that are given are done gently but with crystal clarity. Readings and comments are not rushed but delivered in a cadence that can be followed by English speakers of all levels and in a tone that is inviting and puts us all at ease.

This careful selection of words, and the minimalist approach to the role that the spoken word plays in the worship service, provides more holy space for us all. We the worshipers are better able to receive what God has to say. The measured pace helps my anxious mind slow down; I am less inclined to spring into critique mode and am better able to ponder and digest what I am hearing.

What if I weighed my words as carefully? I'm considering this question not just for the worship services I lead but for the conversations I'm part of on a daily basis. Is it possible that fewer words could have a greater impact than many? Our contemporary culture's habits of discourse would not welcome this suggestion, as everyone everywhere has something to say. And that "everyone" includes me.

Our conviction about protecting the right to freedom of speech is very much a part of this. I have the freedom to say what I want, so when I read a post on social media, I often feel an acute temptation to respond. My urge to add my witty two cents or to steer the conversation in a particular direction may seem completely benign to me. But in truth, every word I post is a word that draws attention to myself—to my voice, to my right to express myself.

It behooves us all to tap the brakes and consider how we are using our words and why. Perhaps I should have the word *wheesht* printed out and taped above my computer screen: *STOP . . . step back and evaluate before you push that button. Are the words you are about to share with the world really that necessary?*

In her book *Wisdom Distilled from the Daily*, Benedictine sister Joan Chittister sheds light on the current disturbing tendency toward narcissism, the symptoms of which include "a grandiose and exaggerated sense of self-importance; preoccupation with fantasies of success; exhibitionism and insatiable attention-getting maneuvers;

disdain or disproportionate rage in the face of criticism; a sense of entitlement that undermines any hope for success in personal relationships; talk that is more self-promotion than communication." I can read Chittister's definition and easily assure myself that I am not a narcissist . . .

> Perhaps I should have the word *wheesht* printed out and taped above my computer screen: *STOP . . . step back and evaluate before you push that button. Are the words you are about to share with the world really that necessary?*

until I get to that last phrase about the purpose of my "talk." What *is* the purpose of all those words I'm so eager to speak?

I'm drawn to the advice of Jeremy Taylor, a British scholar in the seventeenth century who was the chaplain to Charles I, therefore earning him scholarly prestige as one of the Caroline Divines. He was a prolific writer of devotional books on Christian living and had this pointed guidance regarding our speech: "Never say anything, directly or indirectly, that will provoke praise or elicit compliments from others. . . . Only remember this: do not let praise for yourself be the design of your conversations."

Taylor's words may seem alien in today's world, when influencers vie for our attention on social media and people compete for likes and shares. The culture we are part of has a great deal to do with our habits of verbal communication. We are socialized by the country we were born in and the families we were raised in to engage in conversation in particular ways. I've noticed this profoundly during the summers I've spent in Northern Ireland with our university students. Whether it be in a restaurant in Belfast or on a beach on the Antrim Coast, our group unwittingly makes it abundantly clear that "the Americans are here." They are not disorderly or rude; they are just loud. They have loud fun, loud conversations, and loud exclamations, in stark contrast to a culture that in general is quite reserved. Northern Irish folks are kind, authentically warm, and hospitable, but it is all offered at a comparatively low volume.

Then the day comes to board our plane and fly back to the United States. Before we even buckle our seat belts, we are aware that we are back in the presence of Americans—others who, like us, are headed back home. It's not only because their accents are different. Americans are simply louder than the British travelers around them. Having spent more than a month away from our louder culture, we become quite fond of the Northern Irish way of expressing things in a gentler way. The contrast is a bit jarring.

My point here is not to imply that Americans need to change the way they express themselves. My point is that we should pay it more mind. We should recognize the amount of space our words and volume take up and how it affects those around us, both positively and negatively.

The services on Iona pointedly remind me: just because I *can* say something doesn't mean that I should. Just because I have the freedom to say what's on my mind doesn't mean it's a good idea. If I do not take more care with my words, the "noise" I inject into the world can make it more difficult for others to hear God. My words, whether audible or in print, take up a lot of space.

I need to *wheesht*, to be quiet enough to honestly assess if my verbal and written words are superfluous, potentially harmful, or rooted in my own pride.

Monastic communities are built on this kind of humility, having learned over the course of centuries that our insistence on making our voices heard can prevent others from hearing God's voice. There is a spiritual principle at work here, a caution sign. In the New Testament, James, the brother of Jesus, devoted much of his writing to the destructive nature of speech. He wrote that the tongue, while small, can wreak havoc: "Consider what a great forest is set on fire by a small spark," James said by way of analogy (James 3:5).

I have noticed that in an effort to contribute something helpful to discussion, I sometimes swoop into the conversation with a grandiose statement, even if I have no idea what I am talking about. In the middle of a comment, I begin to feel the dissonance within me: *I am yammering on for no other reason than to be heard, to be recognized, to be seen as smart or clever in the eyes of others.* It's self-deception of the first degree.

What does it look like to be a person who generates peace rather than noise?

I always come home from Great Britain with a new awareness of how much I rely on my car. This, of course, has ramifications such as carbon emissions and other environmental effects that are directly related to how much we drive. On Iona, only residents are allowed to have vehicles, so slowdowns are more likely due to a wayward sheep in the middle of the road than traffic. I am not suggesting that this way of life is readily transferable from a tiny island to the highly populated United States. It's just a contrast worth noting. On Iona, there is still the presence of essential services: the red Royal Mail vans that come and go, the ongoing restoration efforts at the abbey, the ferry appearing at the jetty every hour or so. But apart from that, there's not much human noise to report. (Though I did find it amusing on a recent visit to witness a small bulldozer hauling great heaps of seaweed collected from the shore of Martyr's Bay and dumping it in a pile at the Argyll Hotel's organic garden. Apparently, seaweed is a good fertilizer.)

What does it look like to be a person who generates peace rather than noise?

The quiet temperament of Iona goes deeper than the lack of noise. In the same way that even the most raucous tourists will instinctively lower their voices to a hush as they enter Notre Dame or Westminster Abbey, there is a quieting that happens to visitors as they step off the ferry. It is the natural response when one enters a cathedral. And in many ways, that's exactly what Iona is: an island sanctuary where more words are not needed, only more attention to the Word that has been spoken there over many centuries. The need to speak, to proclaim, to defend oneself and one's positions is mysteriously reduced.

I'm slowly learning to feel less urgency to make my voice heard. This might seem a contradiction to the biblical call to speak out against injustice. On the contrary, the more I *wheesht*, the more I am able to discern when to listen (James says to be quick about it) and when to speak or be angry (James says to be slow about it). Silence leads to wisdom.

There is an old prayer in the Psalms that has been a companion of mine for as long as I can remember: "Set a guard over my mouth, Lord; keep watch over the door of my lips" (Psalm 141:3). While there are occasions for thinking out loud and verbally processing the data that is flying into my brain at the speed of sound, I need wise discernment to know exactly when those times are. Our words can be every bit as hurtful as sticks and stones, despite the conventional wisdom of my childhood. I need someone wise who will close the door of the coop before the crazed and impulsive chickens in my brain go rogue, bringing unnecessary commotion to the neighborhood.

The Psalmist's prayer has been answered numerous times for me. God nudges me in the ribs, urging me to stop and consider what the implications of my words are before pushing that send button. Or to let someone else's voice have a chance to be heard before mine. Or perhaps to dare to ponder, *What would happen if I didn't say anything?* Instead of verbally jumping into the fray, what if I give way to the very real possibility that my brilliant contribution may not be helpful at all?

Our compulsion to fill every empty space with noise is worth examining. What is it about silence that makes us twitchy? If an argument is posed, either in person or online, we feel compelled to respond, even when we know that the result is rarely beneficial to either party. If we come home to a quiet house, we automatically respond to the impulse to insert some kind of noise—a television, a stereo, a podcast—even when our bodies are telling us to rest and recover from a demanding day. If we have free space on our calendar, we are quick to fill it with any number of good things, like spending time with friends or taking up an exercise program, because we feel it is indulgent to leave that time unclaimed. It is easier to fill those empty spaces than consider the ironic notion that *absence* can lead us to *presence.*

My youngest daughter recently shared a powerful phrase with me that had been given to her by a woman she admired: "*No* is a freedom word." These are words worthy of full consideration: No *is a freedom word*. Not only does a confident *no* help to keep us from becoming overcommitted and perpetually fatigued, but it also creates a humbling space where we are not in the center of the action. *No* says that it is okay to not be all things to all people all the time. *No* might be one of the most positive words we can utter, a declaration of conviction, a refusal to give in to external pressures that do not give us life but do quite the opposite.

Saying no now and then gives us the time and space to get in touch with who we are called to be in this world. I simply cannot know the genuine answer to that question if my default is to say yes to every request, every opportunity, every voice that demands my attention. When I cave in to those with the intention to please, I experience the opposite of freedom. I am more likely to become who others expect me to be rather than who God has created me to be in the world.

To counteract those external demands requires simple but repeated choices every day. I can say no to the input of media when I get home from work—even for a few minutes—so I can listen to my life, enjoying a respite of *wheesht*. I can sit for a few luxurious moments, take a breath, and be grateful for whatever kind of day it has been. I can embrace the silence long enough to receive the gift of God's presence, a presence that I often overlook in the frantic pace of a typical day. I can gradually learn to appreciate the pure delight of a few moments filled with . . . *nothing*.

Iona has helped train me for this. The more I walk its sacred paths, take notice of the wild orchids waving in the wind, sit on a rock and see the Isle of Skye peeking out from the north, or pat a Highland calf on the head, the more I simply lose the compulsion to fill empty space with my ideas, commitments, or words.

That space is already filled with meaning beyond words.

QUESTIONS FOR SPIRITUAL DIRECTION

1. *When have you felt a deep, calming silence? Where were you when you experienced that?*
2. *Next time you feel the urgency to speak, ask: Do I bring ideas and perspectives that are helpful, or am I just indulging in the opportunity to be front and center?*
3. *How can you know with greater certainty that your words are improving on silence?*

11

BELL

Letting Go

We are able to truly see when we see the earth
from below rather than from above.
　　　—Marlena Graves, *The Way Up Is Down*

Every night at around 8:50, the great bell in the tower
of the abbey sends out a call across Iona, a throwback
to monastic days when monks relied on it to keep
them on schedule for community prayers. I love the
sound as it echoes through the village, bouncing off
the ledges of the Isle of Mull just across the water,
whose pink granite ledges grow ever rosier as the sun
makes its way to the horizon. The sound of the bell
each night triggers an internal process of prepara-
tion, a Pavlovian response: it is time for worship,

so I'd best put my feet on the path and head for the abbey.

Now and then, I've arrived at the abbey early enough to watch the appointed bell ringer call people to worship. The long rope hangs from the bell in its lofty alcove down to the abbey floor, visible to all because of its placement immediately behind the lectern. With a great tug, the bell ringer pulls the rope down, then lets the weight of the bell draw it back up through their hands before they pull again. *Gong . . . gong . . . gong . . .* and as if by magic, folks on the island emerge from their hotels and homes and begin making their way to the service.

On the first night of a recent visit, I found myself walking through the abbey's aging wooden doors well before the great bell sent out its call. I sat directly in front of the lectern and eagerly watched for the evening's bell ringer to take their place. Soon it became clear that the one selected for the role that night was a young man who bore the unmistakable characteristics of Down syndrome. I watched him make his way slowly but purposefully to the bell's rope, and I began to experience no small amount of anxiety. I seriously questioned whether he would be able to carry out such an important responsibility. The uneasiness I felt at that moment embarrasses me now. Who put me in charge of the service? When was I given the ability to know, from merely a glance, what a person is capable of and what they may not be capable of?

As a campus minister, I essentially create and lead worship services for a living, serving on a team that creates two to three worship services each week for a campus of more than a thousand students, faculty, and staff. I've been doing it for over twenty years, which means I'm intimately involved in overseeing more worship services than many pastors are. When I do the math, I figure that I've helped plan and execute something like 1,760 chapel services over my years at the university.

Designing a worship service is creative and holy work. I love the challenge of creating an environment that will help worshipers escape the distractions of their daily lives and come together as a body. I consider it an honor to provide resources that will help our campus community love God and each other. Sometimes it goes really well; other times it does not. During those times, we chalk it up as a learning experience and trust that the Holy Spirit is still able to work through our imperfect leadership.

That evening in the abbey worship service, my worship-planning self was on high alert. My eyes were fixed on the young man with Down syndrome as he stepped forward and took hold of the bell's long rope. I quietly fretted: Had they given him sufficient time to practice? Who would manage the universal discomfort of the congregation if something went awry?

At last he gave the first great pull . . . and a jolt of awareness snapped me to attention. I felt an inner surge of heat move from my neck to the top of my forehead, the kind of sensation that comes when I have been scolded or embarrassed or when I've discovered how very wrong I am. Because, of course, the young man did just fine. He did more than fine; he rang the bell perfectly.

The next night it became clear that this young man not only was the bell ringer for the first night of the week but would be for the rest of my stay. Each night after that, I watched him step up to the rope at just the right time, somewhere around 8:50 p.m., and with the technique of an expert bell ringer, give it a great yank—over and over, with just the right amount of silent space in between each ring and just the right number of times. He rang it with abandon and confidence, as if ringing the bell at Iona Abbey was the most important responsibility any person could be given.

I watched this young man that entire week, not only when he rang the bell but as he participated in the Iona Community, where he was clearly much loved. He helped pass the communion elements during Thursday night's Eucharist service. He shared his contagious smile and hugs with his friends. His presence proved to be the perfect addition to the worship services, a vital element that helped each of us pay attention to the movement of the Spirit.

I once heard a popular recording artist confess that he is no longer able to listen to recordings of music anymore. Not just to his music but to *any* music. I guess when you record music for a living and become something of an expert in it, you find you can't listen to a recording without picking it apart, bit by bit, making it impossible to enjoy the music. The ability to appreciate someone else's creativity, design, and unique expression is stolen simply because of your own experience. It becomes impossible to just sit back and enjoy.

Likewise, there is a disturbing side effect that comes from being "in charge" of so many worship services: it can make sitting through other church services difficult, even upsetting at times. Like that recording artist, I have to fight the urge to analyze everything, from the order of the service and the way the sanctuary is set up, to the songs that are chosen and how they are led, and on and on.

There is a fine line between working for good results and holding too tightly to control. Wisdom and humility are needed to help us recognize what our role is at any given time. That first night at the abbey service, I had absolutely no leadership responsibilities; I was simply a guest among many others who were visiting the island. Yet I easily slid into an unhealthy and habitual posture of control.

As it was, the only responsibility I had—if any— was to pay attention and watch for the image of God. The only responsibility I had was to pay attention to that image clearly and beautifully displayed in the joyful service of a young man I feared might fail. I'm so glad the Iona Community wisely thought otherwise.

Iona, my island spiritual director, has brought me face-to-face many times with my desire for control— even my insistence on it. I am forced to admit a compulsion that, if left unattended, would rob me of the joy of being led. I need to let go of this impulse and just let the bell ring.

A few years ago, I intentionally created an itinerary that put me on Iona for eight days before my pilgrimage group was scheduled to join me—eight glorious days for this introvert to write, explore, pray, and be still. I loved the idea of having plenty of quiet time in my own private space with a good book, a hot cup of tea, and the ocean pulsing outside my window. I happily counted the days until my solo adventure.

> There is a fine line between working for good results and holding too tightly to control. Wisdom and humility are needed to help us recognize what our role is at any given time.

When my departure date came, and I finally arrived at Glasgow International Airport, my luggage, unfortunately, did not. I remember standing at baggage claim in a jet-lagged stupor and staring at the empty luggage carousel, which circled around and around as if to tell me, "You can watch all day, Tracy; it's not here."

I only had what was critical for my long flight: my computer, my journal, a waterproof jacket, and some motion sickness medication. This experience of losing luggage is one that most travelers have had at one time or another (it also happened on my honeymoon). When this happens, it is most often due to a failed connection somewhere along the way. The luggage usually arrives on the next flight and is delivered to your place of residence or accommodation no later than the next day.

This is not possible when Iona is your final destination, because it takes a whole day and four different modes of transportation for a human to get there from Glasgow: train, ferry, bus, and ferry—in that order and according to a very particular schedule. After a quick chat with a chipper Glaswegian luggage handler, it became painfully clear that not only would I not get my luggage that day, or even the next day, but I would likely not get it for three or four.

I had one afternoon in Glasgow before beginning my journey to Iona the next morning, one afternoon to figure out what I needed to get me through several days on a remote island without my luggage. Glasgow is a cosmopolitan city, so I knew I could find what I needed—at a price, of course. Iona, by contrast, has very little in the way of practical shopping. If all I needed were some excellent books, a gorgeous wool sweater, and a stuffed puffin, I'd be in fine shape. Essentials like, say, underwear or basic cosmetics are simply not available. And no, Amazon delivery is not an option—at least not any time soon.

I did a quick shopping spree in the Buchanan Galleries mall that afternoon for what was essential. The next morning, I boarded the train with my backpack, a new floral tote full of basic toiletries, and a shopping bag with two T-shirts, a pair of beige trousers, and a packet of underwear. When I finally arrived on Iona, I splurged and bought a few pairs of whimsical socks from the gift shop (which were totally worth it). Thank goodness no one expects visitors to be fashion-forward there.

I definitely had less baggage to haul up the mile-long path to the north end where my bothy sat.

Curiously, the next few luggage-free days (it turned out to be five, not three or four) in my wee shepherd's hut felt somehow . . . *lighter* to me. Without my suitcase, I had more room in the bothy. I learned to be okay with hair that dried naturally. (Why I ever fuss with my hair at all on Iona is the real question. The wind will greet you with a strong embrace at some point during the day, making it all pointless anyway.) I didn't need to contemplate what I would wear each day because I had so few choices. It proved to be an exercise in determining what was essential in life, of relinquishment, even self-denial. I discovered new ways of following God as I let go of my will, surrendering any demand that my life contain certain things and experiences.

When my suitcase did get delivered to the island, I sort of begrudged its arrival. Now there was more stuff to manage again. It hadn't taken long for me to enjoy the lightness of having less.

Learning that I could do without a lot of things and still be content was a rewarding experience, but in the end, it was not the most important lesson Iona had for me. What I really learned goes back to the abbey bell and my tendency to want *control*. Not every worship service is mine to direct; I need to chill out and know that all will be well. I most definitely cannot control every element of my travel . . . or my work . . . or my life. Things do not always go the way I want them to. I don't get to ring the bell, I sometimes lose my luggage, flights are often late or canceled, even when I've planned my itinerary carefully. The inconveniences of life are plain irritating, but they offer lessons in letting go of inflexibility, pride, and arrogance. Iona has challenged me to abdicate not only more of the stuff that can control me—all the things I imagine I need—but the things I want to control. Which is pretty much everything.

There's an ancient hymn in Philippians 2 that speaks of the *kenosis* of Christ, the "emptying" that Jesus displayed. He willingly renounced certain rights and privileges that were undeniably his as the Son of God. He showed us what it is to let go of control, to be responsive to the will of God. Eugene Peterson translated this passage like this:

> Iona has challenged me to abdicate not only more of the stuff that can control me—all the things I imagine I need—but the things I want to control. Which is pretty much everything.

Think of yourselves the way Christ Jesus thought of himself. He had equal status with God but didn't think so much of himself that he had to cling to the advantages of that status no matter what. Not at all. When the time came, he set aside the privileges of deity and took on the status of a slave, became *human*! Having become human, he stayed human. It was an incredibly humbling process. He didn't claim special privileges. Instead, he lived a selfless, obedient life and then died a selfless, obedient death—and the worst kind of death at that—a crucifixion. (Philippians 2:5–8 MSG)

My experiences on Iona have taught me many things, each deeply rooted in biblical truths. Lessons like *your life is not your own* and *when you're willing to let go of your life, you will find it*. These are words worth listening to, whether I am on a remote holy island or walking an Arkansas country lane. They steady me when I'm grasping for control. They breathe life into my weary soul when I've spent way too much time *doing* and very little time *doing nothing*.

They invite me once again into the joy of living lightly.

QUESTIONS FOR SPIRITUAL DIRECTION

1. *Is there something or someone God might be asking you to hold lightly? What would it look like if you relinquished control?*
2. *Are there things you own that make life feel heavier rather than lighter?*

12

HARP

Beauty on Purpose

You see the world as a dark, messy place that needs rearranging, and with all that light shooting out of your pores you're just the person to do it.

— Andrew Peterson, *Adorning the Dark*

In the summer of 2016, I recognized a woman who came through the front door of the Iona hostel. She had a kind face, older than mine by about a decade, her gray hair blown about by the Iona wind. She wore a fleece jacket that matched her cornflower-blue eyes. I remembered her because, just the day before, as I was putting my grapes and cheese in the hostel refrigerator, she sat in the hostel common room contentedly playing a Celtic harp.

Under normal circumstances, my natural introversion makes initiating conversations a bit awkward. Somehow, that obstacle completely dissipates when I'm on Iona. Its culture and setting have nurtured such a deep curiosity in me for anything having to do with the island that my self-consciousness evaporates. I become eager to connect, especially with those who call Scotland or England their home. Such conversations routinely bear fruit that is deeply satisfying to me: an inspiring story is shared, a common connection discovered, a kinship forged.

This is why it was easy for me to initiate a conversation with the woman in the blue fleece jacket. I simply told her I had heard her playing her harp in the common room the day before and confessed my long-held, secret dream of learning to play the Celtic harp—which is a much smaller version of the harp typically seen on a symphonic stage. For me, the lilting tone of the Celtic harp evokes all my fond memories of green days in Ireland and Scotland. Learning to play the Celtic harp has always seemed like a good idea. (That's as far as it's ever gotten, of course; I have a lot of good ideas like that.)

As I've noted, we Americans can be a lot to handle for the stereotypically understated Brits. This is especially true amid the peace of Iona, where the volume of life is generally turned down—an andante tempo in comparison to the allegro of the States. When I make the acquaintance of someone on Iona, I can come off as a bit starstruck in my eagerness to learn what it's like to, say, raise Highland cattle, make Celtic jewelry, live with the Iona Community, or own the Argyll Hotel. I have to work hard to tone down my enthusiasm, lest I unwittingly put off the new acquaintance I'm secretly hoping will be my new best friend.

This woman, Julie, received my curiosity warmly. With no pretense whatsoever, she promptly offered to come up the path to the bothy to play her harp for me. I eagerly agreed, and we made a plan.

When Julie knocked on my door later that afternoon, only then did I realize what our meeting had required of her: she'd had to lug her harp up the incline of stone steps in order to meet me. I opened the door and promptly apologized for my presumption (we could have met down at the hostel!).

"Oh, I'm used to it!" she said, smiling, the corners of her eyes crinkling. I was grateful for her graciousness. The two of us and the harp squeezed our way into the bothy, where we sat down across from a window framing a perfect landscape of long grasses, blue sky, and the surging Atlantic.

First, we talked. (I think I failed to fulfill the first rule of British hospitality: tea.) I wanted to hear all about her experience with her harp. Now it was Julie's opportunity to be the enthusiastic one. She spoke easily about her love for playing the harp and the ways she has seen it touch human hearts—children, mostly, but also nursing home residents.

"It is remarkable how this soothing music can bring peace to someone who is otherwise agitated, or suffering, or anxious," she said.

Julie also spoke about the outcome of the recent Brexit vote, expressing her distress. We shared our common concerns about the divisions our respective countries were experiencing about all manner of issues, the plight of refugees being one of them.

"The people who voted to leave the EU did so because of fear," she said firmly. "And people who are fearful are generally those who have not traveled, who have not seen the world in ways that help them understand other people." This seemed a valid point.

I think of the college students I work with and how we have evidence that their anxiety levels are rising at an alarming rate. Our campus counseling center tells us their client load has increased substantially. Some of that we can be grateful for, knowing that the stigma that once surrounded therapy has substantially decreased; if our students need help, they feel freer to do so, and that is a good and healthy thing. What is most concerning is that the period of their lives typically marked by excitement and hope for the future is instead being hijacked by intense anxiety. Consider the challenges young people face today: the constant comparison that social media encourages; the addiction to screens and devices that make it harder for young adults to "self-soothe" and self-regulate; the pressure to secure a solid job as soon as possible, particularly with the rising level of student debt they incur while in university. Add to that the chaotic state of the world, issues of identity, and the big spiritual questions that we expect to arise between the ages of eighteen and twenty-two. No wonder anxiety is growing.

Author and monk Thomas Merton put a fine point on it: anxiety is "the fruit of unanswered questions."

In spite of the worries of the world, there in the bothy was Julie from Cornwall singing "Alleluia" over and over as Pachelbel's Canon bubbled from her harp. The gentle notes slid out the bothy window and over Iona's western shore, like a mother pulling the covers up under the chin of her sleeping child. Julie sang and played without a hint of self-consciousness.

After an hour or so together, I felt compelled to release her back into the beauty of a perfect Iona day. She packed up her harp and stepped out the door and down the bothy steps. "It's up to us to rehumanize the world," she said with a smile. I felt I'd been the one who had been rehumanized that day. What a vision—to do what we can to help human beings realize our identity as bearers of the image of God.

Two women, strangers, together for a moment in a metal hut on a tiny island at the edge of the world. A space of gentle peace. She left me with some wisdom that I've

In spite of the worries of the world, there in the bothy was Julie from Cornwall singing Alleluia over and over as Pachelbel's Canon bubbled from her harp. The gentle notes slid out the bothy window and over Iona's western shore.

After she packed up her harp, she stepped out the door and down the bothy steps. "It's up to us to rehumanize the world," she said with a smile.

heard many times: "None of us can do great things, but we can all do small things with great love."

Being on Iona has a way of helping me better understand the role I play in the world—a role that has far deeper dimensions than the tasks I perform or the title I may hold.

We read in Genesis that, from the very beginning, God invited human beings to be colaborers with him: to take care of the garden, to give names to all the animals. Humanity was charged with a creative task by our Creator. Iona's natural beauty affirms this calling at every turn, especially in light of our prideful rejection of God's holy ways from the beginning of Creation.

As we explore what we are called to do with our lives, here's a way to start: add some beauty to this world, big heaping scoops of it. Everyone can do it, and everyone should. Leaning into that longing will produce a beauty that heals, a beauty that ushers us into the presence of God. This kind of beauty "comes in small inspirations" and brings "redemption to our lives and our work," as Sara Groves expresses in a song I rediscovered during my week in the bothy. It became the soundtrack for that week, and years later the chorus still plays in my mind, over and over: "I want to add to the beauty / To tell a better story." When we do this, when we add to the beauty, we are reinvited to participate in God's creative, restorative, nurturing work.

Artist Makoto Fujimura says, "In anything we make, we bring our creative energies, but we are always acting in stewardship of something that we have been given." This is an insightful way of helping us understand the motivation behind adding beauty to the world. We give because we have received. Our contribution of beauty, in whatever form it might take, is ultimately a response of gratitude. I remember that when I learned I was pregnant with my first child, who would also be the first grandchild on both sides of the family, one of my first thoughts was how pleased I was to be able to give this gift to my parents and to my husband's parents—people who had given us so much. I had no doubt that this child would bring endless delight to her grandparents, an idea that made my thankful heart swell.

Beauty is what our world is hungry for, for it serves as a channel of God's love and grace for us. I sense that love in the presence of inspiring art, in the embrace of a much-loved child, or as I'm served delicious edible masterpieces created by a friend. This kind of beauty serves an essential role in our mental and spiritual health, especially in times of great distress in the world. Our small contributions of beauty, like Julie's simple gift of music, are vehicles of hope and light.

There are so many ways this can happen, simply and naturally:

We can write a poem that prompts a reader to follow the Spirit of God in new ways, like Shaw's poem led me to Iona.

We can be practitioners of *kairos* and sacred quietness in a world that is frantic and noisy.

We can be a soul friend; we can listen.

We can welcome, honor, and receive anyone, everyone.

We can send a book to a friend.

We can remind each other to be braver.

We can be an advocate for those who have no voice.

We can be a soul friend; we can listen.

We can welcome, honor, and receive anyone, everyone.

We can send a book to a friend.

We can remind each other to be braver.

We can play a harp for children.

Out of hearts full of gratitude, we can make our contribution of beauty in meaningful ways that point "backward and outward and forward to our ultimate Source and Sustainer," as Fujimura puts it.

If we want to add beauty to the world, sometimes it will demand hard things of us. Sometimes we will first need to step bravely in and remove something unpleasant, or even offensive, in order to clear the way for a better story.

Each fall, our campus ministries team hosts a massive retreat for several hundred university students and staff members who want to hit the spiritual and emotional reset button before the semester gets too far ahead of us. We meet at a local camp that's equipped with everything we need for adventure, accommodation, and space for worship and learning from an invited guest. Our terrific team of student leaders does most of the hard work—staff like me come along, offer a bit of guidance, and basically just cheer them on.

On one of those retreat afternoons, we had just finished lunch. It was free time, and I was hanging around the area in front of our cabin with a couple of those student leaders, chatting unhurriedly, enjoying a few responsibility-free hours. As we did, my eyes were drawn to a car in the nearby lot. The back of the vehicle was covered in bumper stickers that made hateful and discriminatory proclamations. There were images of guns and nationalistic statements aplenty; the car was an assault weapon of another kind.

I gently pointed it out to the students I was with, wondering aloud about its owner. "It's my sister's," said one of my leaders sheepishly. She was just borrowing the car for the weekend; she promptly clarified that she did not agree with the extreme message the bumper stickers were declaring. We talked about it for a moment, giving her the time to think out loud with us. I found the bumper stickers completely inappropriate, but I didn't want my student to feel chastised; it wasn't her car, after all.

Later that afternoon, as I was resting in our cabin, I heard some movement in the parking lot just outside the window. I peeked through the curtains to see my student leader tearing the stickers off her sister's car with determination. I never mentioned it to her. I probably should have, because I was proud of her. She had clearly been doing some thinking about the negative effect those stickers would have on anyone following that car and wanted to clear them away to create space for a better story.

I hope she and her sister had an honest conversation later that weekend and that her action created a new clean space for something better—not just on the car but in their relationship as sisters.

Beauty is restorative. It has a way of breathing life into despairing people and dark places. Our contributions may seem small and inconsequential, but Jesus reminds us that the smallest seed can grow to be a tree so big that birds will come and make their nests in it. It's unlikely that I will ever make a discovery or create art that gets the entire world's attention, but I can open myself up to grace and growth so that birds of all kinds can feel most welcome to come and nest.

QUESTIONS FOR SPIRITUAL DIRECTION

1. If a friend or family member were asked about you, what would they say is one way you add beauty to the world?

2. What are some places that are crying out for the beauty you have to offer?

3. When is the last time someone added beauty to your life in a meaningful way? What difference did it make for you?

EPILOGUE

Creating Sanctuary

> A cathedral is not only a place to which people
> come. It is also a place through which they go,
> and from which they emerge renewed. It is a
> place of integration, between people and with
> God; not in order to escape from the world
> around, but rather to renew commitment to it.
> —Stephen Platten and Christopher Lewis,
> *Flagships of the Spirit*

I recently returned from one of the more hidden yet
essential sacred spaces in our world today: the hospital chapel.

It was New Year's Eve, and my sister, Wendy, was
scheduled for a procedure. She and I have an unspoken agreement to serve as chauffeur for each other
whenever this sort of medical attention is needed,

so I picked her up that morning and we drove to our local hospital.

She checked in at the front desk, and suddenly we were met by Deacon Gary, a gentleman with a clerical collar and a face as kind as Santa's. He was from Wendy's church and came to pray with her before she went in for surgery. I'm sure that meant a great deal to my sister. He could not have known how much it meant to me.

After some small talk, the time drew near for Wendy to be called back to surgery. Had I been Gary, I would simply have brought our circle of three in a bit tighter and led us in prayer right there in the waiting room, and that would have been right and enough. But Gary, in full deacon mode, gently suggested we move to the hospital chapel, just a few steps down the hall.

We relocated to the little room, a large stained-glass image of Jesus praying in Gethsemane occupying the better part of the wall on our left. Gary pulled a small prayer book from his jacket pocket and asked if I'd hold his tiny decanter of holy oil. It was silver and round and sat in my palm like a smooth stone; it bore the engraved Greek letters of alpha and omega.

He led us in prayer for my sister. That prayer, the chapel, the oil, our circle of three—everything coalesced into a holy moment. This was no superstitious exercise, sending Wendy off to surgery with fingers crossed. On the contrary, our five minutes together consecrated that space as sacred. It became a sanctuary, a place to be with God. You might even say it was a place to *coorie in*. The word *sanctuary*, after all, is easily replaced by such synonyms as

haven
harbor
shelter
retreat
refuge

When God calls us into the sanctuary, he is not only calling us to a holy place; he is calling us to himself. The Psalms call God "an ever-present help in trouble" (Psalm 46:1). In fact, the word *refuge* is used forty-three times in the Psalms alone, each time with reference to God.

I used that word earlier to describe Iona, saying that to step onto the shores of Iona is to step into a sanctuary. It is indeed a refuge, a haven. It is a sacred space, made so by the presence and prayers of God's people there over the centuries, just as the hospital chapel was made sacred by our presence, three children of God.

I hang on to Iona for dear life, forcing that sacred space into my pocket. When I am there, I take the same photos I've taken countless times before, because each visit is different. My suitcase is always heavier on the way home than it is on the way there, thanks to the stones I've collected on Columba's Bay, now scattered across nearly every horizontal surface of my office. The walls of that office are sacramentally arrayed with Celtic crosses acquired over the years, joined by framed prints from the Book of Kells, and lining my bookshelves are the works of writers, saints, and travel experts who remind me every single day of the sacred nature of Iona.

Now and then, a first-time visitor in my office will look around and comment, "This office is like a little sanctuary. It's so peaceful." That is just fine with me. I want my guests, especially students, to feel welcomed into a sacred space of grace and peace. There's enough noise and chaos in the world and a myriad of distractions that pull our attention away from God. If the physical setting of my office can help someone be at peace for a few minutes, I am delighted, and if they somehow sense the presence of God, all the better.

I'm convinced that when sacred space is created and made available, there are takers, even in an increasingly secular culture. If there's any lesson Iona has taught me in our journey together, it is that I have the opportunity to share the sacred space of Iona with others. This tiny island has been a vessel of the living, healing waters that flow from the temple of God. It is not mine to keep.

The gift of a place like Iona is that its influence can spread across miles and years as we use our memories of sacred spaces to create other sacred spaces that invite others into refuge. The challenge we face is how to set apart our homes, our workplaces, and even our cars as sanctuaries for the people in our lives, and for ourselves as well.

Some insightful writers have weighed in on this discussion recently. I recommend Tish Harrison Warren's book *Liturgy of the Ordinary: Sacred Practices in Everyday Life*. As the title suggests, it's a book about transforming the most ordinary moments of our days into portals of God's love to us. That desire is what connects the spirituality of the early Christian Celts, the Benedictines, and the Christians of more recent eras living in the Hebrides. Warren's book includes suggested practices to consecrate our everyday moments, like inviting God to teach us how to approach regular daily work as a prayer. "What would it mean to be in your work, yet on your knees?" she asks.

I see this posture lived out every time I visit Subiaco Abbey, the Benedictine monastery here in Arkansas where I am an oblate. The brothers and priests of the abbey live out a seamless rhythm of work and liturgy so that every moment of every day is a prayer. *Ora et labora*—prayer and work—is a guiding principle in these communities. When I witness a monk feeding cattle, or sanding a piece of fine cedar, or weeding a garden, I do not see someone who has laid aside their awareness of God. They may not be standing in the choir stalls for prayer, but their work and prayer are all of a piece; their prayer is their work, and their ordinary daily work is their prayer.

One of my favorite examples of this attitude about prayer and ordinary things comes from the Hebrides:

Bless, O God, my little cow,
Bless, O God, my desire,

Bless Thou my partnership
And the milking of my hands, O God.

I can hardly think of anything more ordinary than milking a cow, while the pray-er of this prayer could not think of anything more holy. Iona has made me alive to the need to create sacred spaces in our world—not in ways that possess but in ways that bless. A good spiritual director takes us by the hand and nudges us into this kind of realized faith, that we might become a living sign of the cross.

The cross that proclaims all humanity as beloved.

The cross that invites and welcomes.

The cross that makes possible a new name and a life of meaning.

The cross that incites wonder and awe before the magnificent work of God.

The cross that is a refuge, a shelter, a sanctuary.

ACKNOWLEDGMENTS

I'm grateful to the many historic voices who have wisely spoken into my life, especially regarding historic Celtic Christianity: St. Patrick, St. Columba, Adomnán (Columba's biographer), and other Celtic saints and contemporary authors like Esther de Waal, Ian Bradley, and many others. My heartfelt gratitude goes to poets Luci Shaw and Kenneth Steven, whose artistry has helped me attend to the Creator and his Creation. I am especially grateful for the gift of Luci's poem "The Holiness of Iona," used in the introduction of this book with her generous permission, and for Kenneth's infectious love for Iona, his generous spirit, and the patient friendship he has offered me. My thanks also go to Noah Mitchell, who served as a reader for chapter 8.

I'm humbled by the opportunity to work with an editor I've admired from afar. Lil Copan, thank you for your inquiry into my work and your willingness to give this writing project a chance. I'm grateful for the editorial expertise of Jana Riess, whose gracious guidance and attention in the tumbling process was just what this book needed in order to shine.

Thanks also to the many pilgrims who have surrendered to my enthusiasm about Iona and have come with me on pilgrimage over the last two decades. Not the least of these pilgrims are my family members, each of whom has been to Iona, some multiple times: my husband, Cary; our daughter Kelsey and her husband, Jordan; our daughter Langley and her husband, Jake; and my sister, Wendy. I hope this book ignites your memories of our holy days on the island together.

To my wee granddaughter, Lizzy Iona, to whom this book is dedicated, be assured that one day, you too will come with me to the sacred isle. Your name requires it, and your grandmother guarantees it.

NOTES

INTRODUCTION

The epigraph comes from a letter from Felix Mendelssohn to Karl Klingemann, "The Islands: Staffa and Iona," Mendelssohn in Scotland, August 8, 1829, https://tinyurl.com/yxjzzvs6.

2 *"How our Celtic blood"*: Madeleine L'Engle and Luci Shaw, *Friends for the Journey* (Ann Arbor, MI: Vine/Servant, 1997), 177–78. Used by permission of the author.

4 *"had a deep understanding"*: Ian Bradley, *Columba, Pilgrim and Penitent* (Glasgow: Wild Goose, 1996), 82.

10 *"If you have ever met"*: Keith R. Anderson and Randy D. Reese, *Spiritual Mentoring: A Guide for Seeking and Giving Direction* (Downers Grove, IL: InterVarsity Press, 1999), 45.

CHAPTER 1: A SACRED ISLAND

17 *"can be filled only"*: Blaise Pascal, *Pensees* (New York: Penguin, 1966), 75.

20 *"It almost hurt me"*: C. S. Lewis, *Till We Have Faces* (Grand Rapids, MI: Eerdmans, 1956), 74–76.

22 *"centuries following Columba's death"*: It was during the final attack that Columban monks took the Book of Kells to Ireland, named so because their final destination was the monastery at Kells, Ireland, that Columba

himself had founded earlier in his life prior to his departure for Iona. For more on the account of the Columban settlement's last years on Iona, see chapter 2 of E. Mairi MacArthur's *Columba's Island: Iona from Past to Present* (Edinburgh: Edinburgh University Press, 1995).

28 *"While the historic Columban"*: According to its website, "The Iona Community is a dispersed Christian ecumenical community working for peace and social justice, rebuilding of community and the renewal of worship." For more information, see https://iona.org.uk/.

33 *"The discontented want"*: James Choung and Ryan Pfeiffer, *Longing for Revival: From Holy Discontent to Breakthrough Faith* (Downers Grove, IL: InterVarsity Press, 2020), 39.

CHAPTER 2: BOTHY

The chapter epigraph is from Henri Nouwen, *The Only Necessary Thing: Living a Prayerful Life* (New York: Crossroad, 1999), 50.

45 *"spiritual practice of creating"*: Cindy Bunch, *Be Kind to Yourself: Releasing Frustrations and Embracing Joy* (Downers Grove, IL: InterVarsity Press, 2020), 23.

48 *"Just to the left"*: Adomnan of Iona, *Life of St Columba* (London: Penguin, 1995), 228.

48 *"discovery of archaeological significance"*: Ken Macdonald, "Scientists Uncover St. Columba's Cell on Iona," BBC News, July 11, 2017, https://tinyurl.com/y27w4yl5.

CHAPTER 3: STAFFA

The chapter epigraph is from John O'Donohue, *To Bless the Space between Us* (New York: Convergent, 2008), 154.

56 *"little brother of the north"*: "Puffin FAQs," Audubon Project Puffin, https://tinyurl.com/y6mdsldy.
56 *"a colony, a puffinry"*: "Puffin," Oceanwide Expeditions, https://tinyurl.com/yyc32yjx.

CHAPTER 4: BRIGHT MOMENTS

The chapter epigraph from Camille Pissarro is quoted in Bonnie Smith Whitehouse, *Afoot and Lighthearted: A Journal for Mindful Walking* (New York: Clarkson Potter, 2019), 63.

77 *"These pure and spontaneous"*: C. S. Lewis, *Letters to Malcolm, Chiefly on Prayer* (New York: Harcourt Brace Jovanovich, 1963), 91.

CHAPTER 5: TUMBLING

97 *"from the work of Ignatius"*: For more on Ignatian spiritual practice, see Mark E. Thibodeaux, *Reimagining the Ignatian Examen: Fresh Ways to Pray from Your Day* (Chicago: Loyola Press, 2015).
99 *"This is a beautiful"*: For more about the Celtic concept of *anamchara*, see Ian Bradley's *Celtic Christian Communities: Live the Tradition* (Kelowna, BC: Northstone, 2000); and Ray Simpson's *Soul-Friendship: Celtic Insights into Spiritual Mentoring* (London: Hodder and Stoughton, 1999).
101 *"inexpressible comfort of"*: George Eliot, as quoted in Bradley, *Celtic Christian Communities*, 111.

102 *"this tool can help us"*: Ian Morgan Cron and Suzanne Sta-
     bile, *The Road Back to You: An Enneagram Journey to Self-
     Discovery* (Downers Grove, IL: InterVarsity Press, 2016), 35.

CHAPTER 6: WHITE STONE

The chapter epigraph is from Antoine de Saint-Exupéry, *The
Little Prince* (New York: Scholastic, 1971), 87.

CHAPTER 8: COLUMBA'S TEARS

The chapter epigraph is a tweet from Dara McAnulty (@natu-
ralistdara), July 20, 2020, https://tinyurl.com/yy4gh8l5.

145 *"1921 Tulsa race riots"*: Allison Keyes, "A Long-Lost Man-
     uscript Contains a Searing Eyewitness Account of the
     Tulsa Race Massacre of 1921," *Smithsonian Magazine* and
     the National Museum of African American History
     and Culture, May 27, 2016, https://tinyurl.com/y3dr9xfu.
147 *"offers faith leaders compelling"*: Matthew Soerens, "How
     Pastors Can Help Their Congregations Address the
     Issue of Immigration," Faith and Leadership, Septem-
     ber 4, 2018, https://tinyurl.com/y3kuv6pl.
148 *"make the imaginative effort"*: Mark Honigsbaum, "Barack
     Obama and the 'Empathy Deficit,'" *Guardian*, January 4,
     2013.
151 *"the first step in"*: Jemar Tisby, *The Color of Compromise: The
     Truth about the American Church's Complicity in Racism*
     (Grand Rapids, MI: Zondervan, 2019), 15.

CHAPTER 9: COORIE IN

The chapter epigraph is from Anne Lamott, *Traveling Mercies: Some Thoughts on Faith* (New York: Pantheon, 1999), 163.

164 *"Mister Rogers made a strategic"*: Christine Jackson, "The Importance of Sweaters and Sneakers in Mr. Rogers's Neighborhood," Rewire, March 20, 2017, https://tinyurl .com/y66geh49. For more on Mister Rogers, see Maxwell King, *The Good Neighbor: The Life and Work of Fred Rogers* (New York: Abrams Press, 2018).

CHAPTER 10: WHEESHT

170 *"importance of silence"*: Tracy Balzer, *Permission to Ponder: Contemplative Wisdom for the Spiritually Distracted* (Abilene, TX: Leafwood, 2015).

172 _*"abbey church has been restored"*: For more information on the history of the abbey, see http://www.iona.org.uk.

175 *"a grandiose and exaggerated"*: Joan Chittister, *Wisdom Distilled from the Daily: Living the Rule of St. Benedict Today* (San Francisco: HarperSanFrancisco, 1990), 55–56.

175 *"Never say anything"*: Richard Foster and James Bryan Smith, *Devotional Classics* (New York: HarperOne, 2005), 270.

CHAPTER 12: HARP

The chapter epigraph is from Andrew Peterson, *Adorning the Dark: Thoughts on Community, Calling, and the Mystery of Making* (Nashville: B&H, 2019), 3.

202 *"anxiety levels are rising"*: Nicole J. LeBlanc and Luana Marques, "Anxiety in College: What We Know and

How to Cope," *Harvard Health Blog*, May 28, 2019, https://tinyurl.com/y7vog9mg.

203 *"fruit of unanswered questions"*: Thomas Merton, *No Man Is an Island* (New York: Houghton Mifflin, 1983), xiii.

205 *"comes in small inspirations"*: Sara Groves, "Add to the Beauty," track 5 on *Add to the Beauty*, Sony BMG, 2005.

206 *"In anything we make"*: Makoto Fujimura, *Culture Care: Reconnecting with Beauty for Our Common Life* (Downers Grove, IL: InterVarsity Press, 2017), 53.

208 *"backward and outward"*: Fujimura, 52.

EPILOGUE

The epigraph is from Stephen Platten and Christopher Lewis, *Flagships of the Spirit*, quoted in Ian Bradley, *Colonies of Heaven: Celtic Christian Communities* (London: Darton, Longman, and Todd, 2000), 31.

218 *"connects the spirituality"*: For more on this, see my book *Thin Places* (Abilene, TX: Leafwood, 2007), as well as Esther de Waal's *The Celtic Way of Prayer* (New York: Random House, 1999).

218 *"What would it mean"*: Tish Harrison Warren, *Liturgy of the Ordinary: Sacred Practices in Everyday Life* (Downers Grove, IL: InterVarsity Press, 2017), 168.

218 *"where I am an oblate"*: *Oblate* is a term meaning "offering" and is a designation for laypeople—men and women, Catholic and Protestant—who want to follow the Benedictine path of spiritual growth and maintain a familial connection to a Benedictine monastery.

218 *"Bless, O God, my little cow"*: Quoted in Balzer, *Thin Places*, 77.